t h e **VOICE**

WORKBOOK

USE YOUR VOICE WITH CONFIDENCE

A n g e l a   C a i n e

*ead*way · Hodder & Stoughton

First published 1991

Typeset by Wearside Tradespools, Fulwell, Sunderland
Printed in Great Britain for the educational publishing division of Hodder and Stoughton Ltd, Mill Road, Dunton Green, Sevenoaks, Kent by Butler & Tanner Ltd.

British Library Cataloguing in Publication Data
Caine, Angela
  The voice workbook.
  1. Voice production. Exercises
  I. Title
  808.5076

  ISBN 0–340–54215–2

For Pat Nicholson and Auntie Joyce

About the Author

Angela Caine trained at the Guildhall School of Music and Drama. At 30 her voice began to deteriorate; she frequently lost her speaking voice and began to sing out of tune. In the opinion of her former teachers the voice was finished. She was advised to give up any idea of performance and become a singing teacher instead. She discovered to her horror that this was the way that many people became teachers of the voice. She also discovered that the drop-out rate for people whose voices had been trained was alarmingly high and if your voice was in good shape after 40 your were doing well and you had probably escaped voice lessons. Angela is now over 50 and the voice has never been better. She lives and works in Norfolk and has just completed a three year training to become a teacher of Alexander Technique. She is one of a team all concerned about and working with the different demands people make on their voices. The team includes a psychologist, a Danish speech therapist, a jazz musician and a yoga teacher, all of whom have Alexander training and have contributed in some way to this book.

Acknowledgements

The exercises in this book are very simple and very effective, due to the patience and tolerance of many guinea pigs who have largely contributed to this simple method of voice work. Many did not realise during their voice lessons that information was being gathered. Among the precious personal securities I have been allowed to tamper with are the way they talked, the language they used and how they performed in public. The work we have done together and the risks they were prepared to take with their voices have cleared away much of the witchcraft currently surrounding the voice. There is no mystery about getting your voice to work for you in a way that pleases you.

When you see yourself in a mirror with a plant on your head and wonder whether you are sane; when you are stationary on the M25 singing a Russian Folk Song and pulling one cheek towards your ear, and you catch sight of the expression on the face in the car next to you, tell yourself that all the following people have been through it and are now quite delighted with the result.

My apologies for giving such a hard time to Pat Nicholson, Vivien Mackie, Michael Mills, Tony Buzan, Bob Rickover, Gill Birley, Andrew Hodge, Sara Jane Morris, Don Burton, Margaret Royle, Claudia Ebersoll, Jan King and Carolyne Roberts.

Special thanks to Gaynor Grimshaw, who edited my typescript before it went to the publisher, and to Anne Gibbens for her translation of the Russian song.

Contents

Introduction

When you hear people speaking with confidence do you think 'Oh I wish I could do that'? When you hear someone singing, do you wish *you* could sing? There is nothing mysterious about singing and speaking well. You will find that out when you work through this book. It will explain how your voice works, and there are easy and often amusing exercises to help strengthen it. Many people assume that a strong voice would be loud, pushy or aggressive but that is not what this scheme of work is about. The book contains all you need to know to turn your voice into a true personal asset. The strong voice can express authority, sympathy, support, and yet remain essentially an expression of 'Yourself'. As that 'Self' grows and develops so the strong voice grows and develops with you so that throughout your life its quality and range will be extending.

Your strong voice talks equally well to one hundred people or one person, adjusting automatically as to pitch, distance and volume. In fact you and your strong voice are so interdependent that you cease to consider your voice as something you possess . . .

'I wish *my* voice were more interesting'

'I had a cold and lost *my* voice'

instead you feel it to be an essential part of *you* operating like a great engine within, affecting, and responding to, everything you do.

Like a great engine, a strong voice is equally at home toiling steadily for hours on end in adverse conditions or performing delicate and sensitive tasks with subtlety and grace.

You do not lose a strong voice because you have an

unusually heavy and exhausting schedule. After such a workload the strong voice requires nothing more recuperative than to have a really good sing to replace its essential oils and release its tensions.

Currently actors have voice lessons and singers have singing lessons. From this one would assume that we have two voices, one that speaks and one that sings. But we have only one voice that both speaks AND sings. In other words, we have one vocal machine that expresses one individuality and the two functions of that vocal machine should have the same quality, a quality uniquely yours.

By helping you to recognise, step by step, what is happening to your voice as you use it, I hope this book will enable you to do anything which involves speaking or singing. Interviews and public presentations do not have to be tense and difficult situations; they should show you at your best and you could enjoy them. Choirs and dramatic societies should provide an opportunity to stretch and expand in every way. It is enormously fulfilling and energising to feel your voice working for you.

Before working on your voice you may well have described the difference between those who could 'present', sing, make speeches and those who couldn't as 'having confidence' or 'having no confidence'. One of the aims of this book is to free people from the idea that confidence is something which you have or have not as one of life's gifts. Confidence can be increased by gaining a life skill. Learning to use your voice is one of the very basic life skills. Build it up, and with it your confidence, by working on the tape in your car whenever there is an opportunity. In the car, you can feel safe from criticism and also use some of the wasted time spent sitting in traffic jams.

Finally, when you are familiar with your voice and have given it a thorough service and maintenance programme, you will find you have a better understanding of how it works. This has a knock on effect. Understanding develops competence. Competence gives you the courage to use what you now recognise as a personal skill. You may now describe yourself as having gained confidence.

Where has singing gone?

No-one seems to be complaining publicly about the decline of singing in all age groups. The media discuss problems of illiteracy, violence, declining standards of behaviour, vandalism. There is never any mention of the seriousness of non-singing. Non-singing is not mentioned by doctors or psychiatrists, nor even in education, as one of the declining activities. Many people don't sing at all. The activity of singing *is* declining. Choirs and music societies are constantly campaigning for young members. Even in large schools choirs are often only made possible by the support of the staff. The weekly singing class for everyone has gone and is replaced by an option. In many schools singing is exclusively an activity within the Music Department. There is less singing at football matches; the band which accompanied the crowd has retired to safety. How many social occasions have you been to lately which ended with a singsong? A gloomy, declining situation I'm afraid – we do not want singing only for the 'singers'; it is a natural endowment we all possess. However, it is not generally known that singing is available to everyone because it is the primary function of the voice. Much of the singing work here is based on my long experience of teaching a variety of 'non-singers' who were enabled to realise that they were, after all, singers and had always been so. **It is not difficult to swap from non-singer to singer.** Singing is an innate human characteristic. Work on singing is based on examining the habits you have built into your voice at home, school and the life you have chosen. Those habits are examined by looking at and listening to the way you sing and speak. You then learn to ask yourself the questions which give you a choice: whether you keep those habits because they are good for you or whether you throw them away because they interfere with the best in you. How far you progress depends entirely on how carefully you look and listen and how frank you are about what you observe. You do not need ideal facilities or large amounts of time, but you do need to answer the questions honestly.

Singers and actors may also find this groundwork useful and it will not interfere with their advanced work. Above all, I intend to show that it can be enjoyable to work on your voice and you can develop real strength by having fun.

Equipment and music

Always work barefoot in very loose clothing: a tracksuit is ideal. If your feet are *very* cold wear socks, but it is better to do some foot exercises to get them warm again.

Collect the equipment below together and keep it all in a heap somewhere accessible.

Equipment

1 **A bean bag.** Make one easily from a plastic bag half filled with beans or peas.

2 **A fairly heavy plant in an enclosed pot.** As you are going to put it on your head it is better if water does not drip out of the bottom.

3 **A music stand.** Books and music are heavy and can overbalance you if you hold them for any length of time. Some of the work requires the book to be still while you move around.

4 **Two or three paperback books** of different thicknesses to provide a variable support for your head on the floor.

5 **A tennis ball, a toothbrush** and **a large towel.**

6 **A full-length mirror.** As this is probably on a wardrobe, mirror work will have to be done there. There will also be work in front of **the 'head and shoulders' bathroom mirror.**

7 **A portable cassette player** to play the work tape and **another in your car.** A Walkman is fine.

8 **A children's story book** with coloured
pictures and large print. An ideal one is
Maurice Sendak's 'Where The Wild Things
Are', a Picture Puffin.
9 **A recipe book** – your favourite one.
10 **A wobble board** and **a balancing board.** You,
or a handy friend, will have to make these.
They are easy and cheap to make and plans
are at the back of this book, on page 208.
11 **A Notebook.** You will use this to jot down
observations and devise a work programme
later on.

Music

All these songs are on side 2 of the tape and can be
learned just by playing the tape and soaking them up.
However, you may become curious about reading the
music and when that happens – not before! – the
following are easily obtained from Chappell & Co Ltd,
50 New Bond Street, London, W1A 2BR. There is no
sex discrimination and no age factor relevant. *Anyone*
can sing *all* these songs. The words are on pages 201–4.

1 **Send In The Clowns**
Music and lyrics by Stephen Sondheim.
2 **My Lord What A Morning**
Negro Spiritual. Any edition will do. The one on the
tape is arranged by H T Burleigh.
3 **Lascia Ch'io Pianga** (Lashya Keeo Peeanga)
by G F Handel in the low key.
4 **S'Wonderful, S'Marvellous**
by George Gershwin.
5 **Drink To Me Only With Thine Eyes**
an Old English Air.

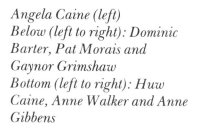

Angela Caine (left)
Below (left to right): Dominic
Barter, Pat Morais and
Gaynor Grimshaw
Bottom (left to right): Huw
Caine, Anne Walker and Anne
Gibbens

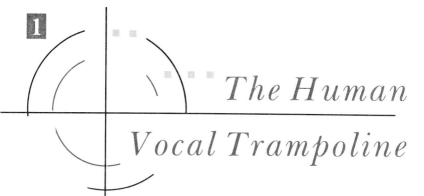

1

The Human Vocal Trampoline

Here is a picture of a trampoline. The gymnast bouncing on it has to rely on its strength, flexibility and spring to gain the upthrust which will enable her to turn somersaults and backflips.

The human vocal trampoline

The **STRENGTH, FLEXIBILITY** and **SPRING** are created by the trampoliner bouncing on whichever section of the mat she chooses. The qualities of strength, flexibility and spring are co-ordinated in the mat, but the source of each is from different parts of the trampoline, as follows:

STRENGTH is provided by the frame.

FLEXIBILITY is provided by the springs which link the frame to the mat.

SPRING is provided by the mat, where the trampoliner lands.

By using the analogy of the trampoline, I can give you a simplified idea of the important vocal equipment which you possess.

The trampoliner needs:	For singing and speaking you need:
FRAME	SKELETON
SPRINGS	MUSCLES
MAT	LARYNX or VOICE BOX

This analogy will also help you to realise that your vocal mechanism is not just in your throat; it is a part of your whole body and mind.

Let's look first at the frame of the human trampoline, which is your skeleton and those muscles that move it about. Here are some exercises to help you to locate and observe it.

Your vocal frame

You may never have considered that the way you stand, how you are balanced, the tension in hands, feet, shoulders and hips, can seriously affect the way that your voice operates for you. These considerations are *much* more important than whether you can read music or have the time to practise every day.

You need to stand in front of a mirror regularly to observe how you stand. We think we know how we stand because we check where arms and legs are by the feelings we have about them, but usually when we are in front of a mirror we are checking hair or clothes, not the body which is inside the clothes. Have a good look before you begin the following exercise so that you can observe any changes afterwards. Shaking your hand, for example, can cause you to lean far over to one side and that is not what we want – but you must **see** that you are doing it before you can correct it.

At first it is embarrassing to watch yourself doing peculiar exercises and there is something in us which tells us we are being selfish or narcissistic to pay so much attention to ourselves. I'm afraid that notion has to be knocked straight on the head. This whole book is about paying attention to yourself in a wholesome and creative way, and enjoying it into the bargain.

EXERCISE • *Shaking out*

'Shakeout' is about getting in touch with hands, arms, shoulders, feet, legs, everything. 'Shakeout' takes about ten minutes.

Shake your fingers and hand off your wrist

Hands and arms

Barefoot, in front of the full-length mirror, begin with one hand and shake your fingers and hand off your wrist. Watch the rest of your body and reduce its involvement to a minimum. Be interested in the various positions in which the hand will waggle.

When you feel really in touch with the circulation in the hand and fingers allow the forearm to join in, mobilising the elbow joint. Mentally disengage it from your upper arm and shoulder to allow the elbow joint maximum freedom. This joint does a great deal of work in the course of a day and playing carelessly is a great relief to it. Finally, having explored every possible waggling of wrist and elbow, allow the upper

Now allow your arm to join in

arm to join in, throwing the arm about everywhere, behind, in front, over your head, away from and across your body.

Notice any cracking and grinding, whether the shoulders feel loose or stiff. Do not try to change that, but decide instead to observe yourself by *listening* to the way your body moves. Do not be too hard on yourself. When thoughts creep in like: 'I'm too stiff', 'I'm too old/tired for this', 'This is stupid', push them out again – do not be judgemental. Answer all of it with: 'Yes, but I'm curious to know what this has to do with my voice, so I'll just get on with it'. Observing the movement of your body is a very important part of voice work. When you have given the whole arm a vigorous shakeout leave it alone, notice the difference, and repeat the procedure with the other arm. You may notice differences between the movement of your two arms. This is quite usual; they generally do quite different jobs. Because you have for so long taken for granted the way in which they operate for you it is very good to make movements which are not habitual.

Feet and legs

Now move your attention to your feet and legs.

Shake one foot, imagining it as another hand on the end of your leg, with the same mobility and flexibility. Really shake it off the end of your leg. This is a good balancing exercise and the rest of your body, including arms and hands, may have to help. If you find this very difficult, steady yourself with one hand on a piece of furniture.

Next join in your lower leg, shaking out the kneecap and the back of the knee, again maintaining your balance: your other foot must work very hard and sometimes jump about to balance you.

Lastly bring in the upper leg and hip joint. Now you can appreciate the weight of a leg as it throws itself about and your whole body will have to do an incredible compensatory dance in order to stay on one foot. Compare the movement of the leg with the movement of the arm. The shoulder joint is the most mobile joint of the whole body, but the hip can be very flexible too. It suffers from continuous walking on hard pavements, or standing for long hours, which reduces its degree of rotation. Notice whether side movements away from the body are harder than forward, backward swings.

Your feet and legs

(Left): Really shake your foot
off the end of your leg
(Below left): Now let your
lower leg join in
(Below right): Now let
everything go . . . voice as well

Shake everything!

Now shake all four limbs together, dancing from foot to foot and flailing legs and arms around. Add the shaking of head, hips, tongue and jaw, so that the whole of you performs an energetic dance.

In the last few seconds before you fall exhausted, let go of any noises you wish to make, as loudly as you can.

This is probably the moment to mention that sooner or later you will be caught doing this or one of the other exercises in this book which cannot be done in the safety of your car. An unsuspecting postman or your nearest and dearest, or, worst of all, your children, will see you dancing, grimacing and apparently having gone 'bananas'. Let them think you have a wasp down your trousers and ignore them!

Shake all your limbs in the air as hard as you can

Rest

Finally flop down on your back and allow this loosened body to sink into the floor as hot butter might sink into toast. Lie stretched out and **rest** as long as you can. Then pick up all four limbs like a dead beetle on its back and shake them all in the air as hard as you can, shaking all parts of your back against the floor and again letting out any noises that come. Keep it up until you think you can't continue, then do it some more and finally collapse back on the floor. Rest again and observe the looseness of arms, legs and neck.

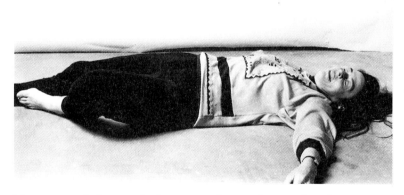

Now rest and observe the looseness of arms, legs and neck

EXERCISE • *Stretching up*

Now stand up. Just stand for a moment and check that you are still in touch with your extremities, the hands and the feet. They are the corner posts of the frame of

your voice trampoline. Stand with your hands
outstretched above you for a moment and look at
yourself in the mirror.

Look at the photographs of people with pots on their heads. It is important that the elbows are taken out to the side and pot is held securely on the top of the head. Try this yourself now. Your back is a strong spring. When you put this heavy plant on top of it, the spring is stimulated causing you to stretch upwards. Visualise this spring whenever I ask you to put a plant on your head throughout this book. Can you feel the effect that holding the weight of the plant pot 'up' has on your height? Try and aim for this feeling every time I ask you to put a plant on your head throughout this book!

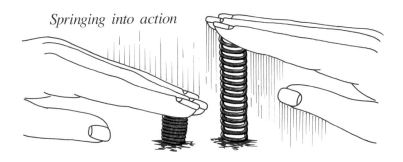

Springing into action

When you feel particularly exercised, balanced and good, try standing on your wobble board (see page 24) to get the feel of it. You will need it later for exercises on the tape. To balance, keep the upper part of your body poised and still. Hips, knees and ankles perform with a deep, slow wobble. When you have practised this sufficiently to become confident, try standing on your wobble board while holding a plant on your head.

Do not attempt the balance board for the moment. Page 168 gives you some advice on using it.

Balancing on your wobble board

Draw an imaginary frame around yourself and superimpose this imaginary frame onto the picture of a trampoline on page 13. You have just been exercising the strong frame of your vocal trampoline, the joints of your skeleton and those muscles which move it about. This increases its potential to strengthen and support your voice. Every part of it needs to be strong and supportive from head down to toes if you are able to sit, walk, hold a book while you talk or sing. The one difference between the frame of an ordinary trampoline and the frame of your vocal trampoline is that *your* frame can move and still remain strong and supportive to the voice. Then, when you stand in front of the mirror you are observing **stillness** of a body which is alert and ready to move, not a body which is **stiff** and cannot move. You are now ready to make your first singing noises.

Your vocal springs

Many people stiffen themselves at the moment when they begin to sing or speak. Because we all have different habits, there are almost as many different patterns of stiffening as there are people. The following simple exercise ensures that, at the moment when silence changes to sound, the spring system of the vocal trampoline is free to operate easily. It is achieved by turning the whole body into one enormous spring.

This exercise will give you a very good, and maybe a very different sensation of the way you start to make a sound.

EXERCISE ❶ *On 'Gah' and 'Lah'*

The exercises on side 1 of the tape are set out so that you can either copy what I do in the pauses provided or compete with me as I speak or sing. Or you can go solo when you feel you want to.

What to do

In this exercise you are going to squat down, hit the floor between your feet, spring up and speak or sing 'gah' or 'lah'.

Notes

It is a good idea to practise hitting the floor before going ahead with the exercise. Use your mirror initially to check all is going well. When you hit the floor, squat down to do so as follows: stand with feet slightly apart, squat, and hit the floor hard with both hands *between* your feet. It is important that your knees move away from each other, froglike, and that your bottom aims for the floor.

You may be stiff in ankles, knees or hips so persevere, kindly. Use a push off the floor to bring you back to standing position.

Now practise this without looking at yourself in the mirror, bearing the following points in mind: it is better if the heels can stay as close to the floor as possible. Look at the floor to decide where you are going to hit and keep watching your hands do it. Imagine something running across the floor which you watch. When it arrives between your feet you squat and crush it. As you squat, aim for a long line from top of head to bottom of spine. Here is a good squat for you to look at:

A good squatting position

No!

Yes!

THE HUMAN VOCAL TRAMPOLINE 27

When you spring back to standing position, maintain the good long line of head and back when you spring up, but don't stiffen. Beware of overbalancing and throwing the head back as you straighten.

Finally, when you spring up, practise pointing at something in the room. Keep your shoulders relaxed with no forward thrust. Elbow need not straighten but finger and eye must be accurate.
Now work with the tape!

This apparently silly exercise is one of the most important in the book. The voice should operate by *springing* into action, but most people do not experience any sensations which would be described as a spring. When I have questioned people with undeveloped voices about how they would describe what they felt when talking or singing I have had all the following answers:

'My throat tightens.'
'My tongue goes all stiff.'
'It's like having asthma, I can't get enough breath.'
'If I talk for a long time my knees hurt . . .
                              my back hurts . . .
                              my neck aches . . .
                              my shoes begin to hurt.'
'I feel exhausted.'
'My throat gets dry.'
'My mouth dries up.'
'I get a sore throat.'

No-one has ever complained about a moving, jumping, springing sensation because if these were experienced singing would be enjoyable.
Exercise 1 on 'gah' and 'lah', then, is to change your attitude towards the voice.

From now on, your voice will
SPRING INTO ACTION as you sing GAH.

Locating your vocal springs

Now you have created a springiness throughout your
whole body you can locate the springs central to the
vocal trampoline. Simple exercises will follow on pages
35–6 to help you find them while singing and talking.
Some of the exercises will use the voice, but some will
be just to remind you how important it is to maintain a
strong and flexible body providing a good frame to
support the springs of the voice. Remember that you
do not talk and sing using just the throat, but all of
you.

Locate the following areas on yourself, prodding
with your fingers where possible and watching in the
mirror, so that you can imagine these areas working as
you talk and sing.

The soft palate

This is the continuation of the roof of your mouth.
Look in the mirror at the back of your mouth for the
uvula which hangs down in the middle of the soft
palate when it is relaxed and disappears when you
yawn. Cut a piece out of a balloon and stretch it
between your hands so that you can pull it into
different shapes with your fingers. The soft palate
behaves in the same way as this balloon, being shaped

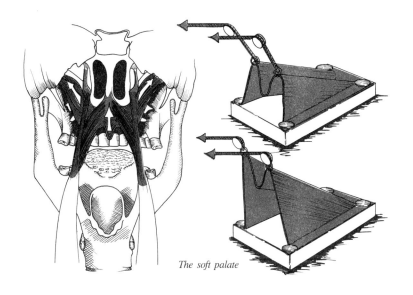

The soft palate

by muscles in the throat to balance nose, mouth and throat spaces as the tongue and throat muscles articulate consonants. You can see your soft palate from in front if you arrange a light so that it shines into your mouth. The diagram shows you what it looks like from behind. Imagine that you are standing on a ledge in the back of the throat, and looking out into the world through your mouth.

The tongue

Put out your tongue as far as you can and you will see about one third of it. Beginning under your chin, just behind the jaw bone, poke and prod about around the front of your neck, meanwhile waggling the tongue

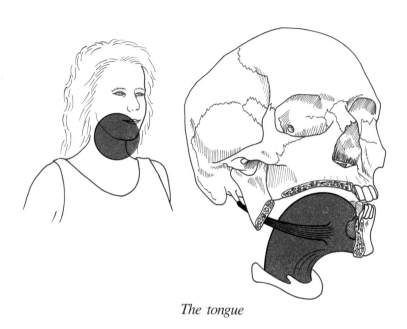

The tongue

about as hard as you can. Open the mouth to do this. Continue down to your collar bone to discover how influential your tongue is on the whole neck area. Prod about also at the back of your jaw, all the way up to your ear and behind it. Test the back and sides of your neck, moving your tongue about as you go.

The diaphragm

This is the one voice spring that everyone seems to know about. Creep your fingers down your breastbone till it ends and find its tip. The front of your diaphragm forms a dome across your body from front to back, beginning here and anchoring into your back just below waist level. It is the main muscle of your

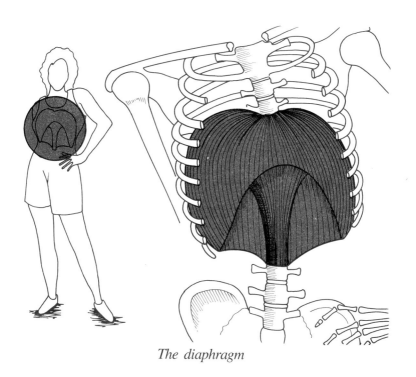

The diaphragm

breathing system but, having said that, for the moment just think of it as the largest and strongest spring that we have located so far.

Pelvic floor

If you put your hand between your legs from the front and then sit on it on a hard chair you will locate three bony areas forming a triangle. The two back ones are your sitting bones. The front bone is the pubic bone. The muscular triangle formed by these three bones is

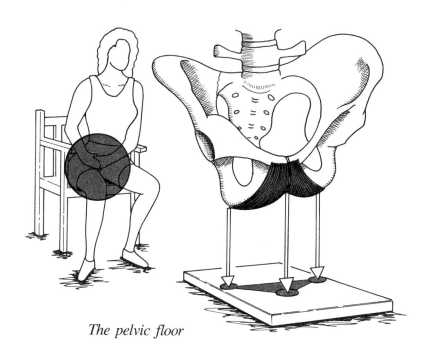

The pelvic floor

your pelvic floor. This area, of course, also contains the genitals, so the pelvic floor is very muscular and strong to support sexual activity.

Omohyoid muscle

Omo refers to the shoulder and hyoid refers to a bone in the throat – the hyoid bone. Make your thumb and

index finger into a horseshoe shape and push the
horseshoe into the throat under the chin. Tip your
head back and swallow (gently). The hyoid bone can be
felt as the top of a set of bony rings as it leaps upwards
to swallow. That is one end of the omohyoid muscle.

Trace your collar bone out from the neck along the
shoulders (keep digging in with your fingers). You will
eventually discover where it joins your shoulder blade:
the other end of your omohyoid muscle is attached to
the shoulder blade. The muscle passes through a loop
at the base of your neck, which forms a pulley. The
result is that as your head turns while you talk and sing
it can adjust to maintain the central position of the
voice box. The voice box is the first two bony rings you
can feel immediately beneath the hyoid bone.

Place one hand on your hyoid bone (lightly this time)
and one on the shoulder depression. Turn the head
and imagine the muscles sliding through a pulley at
the base of your neck. Check this in the mirror,
making sure that your shoulder does not become
involved in the turning of the head. Talk or sing as you
make this movement, 'sending' your shoulder blades
down your back to stabilise the voice mechanism.

These five main springs are directly responsible for
the freedom or lack of it which you experience when
you talk. If only one of them is behaving in a weak or
unco-ordinated fashion you may not sing in tune or
may not be able to enjoy talking. They are not, by any
means, the whole system, but they are certainly your
key springs, and if we work on those, exercising and
co-ordinating them, the whole system will gradually be
activated.

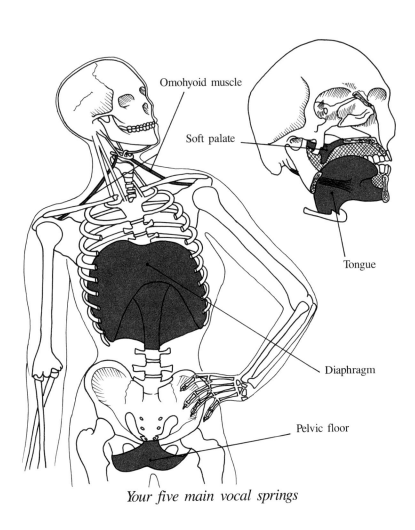

Your five main vocal springs

Your vocal trampoline mat

The bony rings you can feel down the front of your neck are made of cartilage and the first two rings below the hyoid bone form the larynx – or the voice box –

which houses the vocal mechanism – or vocal cords. As the larynx is made of cartilage (like your nails) it is strong but not rigid (as is your skeleton frame). The sounds you make are formed in the larynx by the action of the vocal cords. These cords respond to directions from your imagination.

The spring mechanism of:

> soft palate
> tongue
> diaphragm
> pelvic floor
> omohyoid muscle

which we have just investigated is activated by a demand made on the larynx in its supporting frame, the skeleton. The larynx is in suspension because it needs to move about while we talk and sing. Our role is to maintain an easy but strong posture so that this may happen. Your larynx is in fact the 'mat' of your vocal trampoline.

🔲 EXERCISE ❷ *'Drain noises'*

'Exercise' may seem a strange word to describe the peculiar noises in exercise 2 on the tape. However, it is a foolproof method for locating and investigating the larynx. I call them 'drain' noises and that picture makes them instantly available to everyone. Should you be able to discover new noises, do let me know!

While you are making drain noises, the larynx is leaping about on its flexible springs about as far as it can go in any direction. Drain noises for the larynx allow you to 'bounce' lightly up and down on your vocal trampoline mat – and observe what is happening.

What to do

Make drain noises – listen first to the examples on the tape!

Further work

When you have exhausted your repertoire of noises, repeat it with a hand wrapped round your throat to feel the extent of movement possible to the larynx. Play around with those probing fingers and you will discover the hyoid bone again with the bony rings extending to your collar bone all leaping about forwards, backwards, upwards and downwards.

Now make your drain noises yet again. Feel the movements of your larynx with your hand. Imagine omohyoid, tongue, hyoid bone, soft palate, diaphragm and pelvic floor all coordinating to allow the movement.

Your vocal trampoline

EXERCISE ● *Sing, talking . . . on the floor*

Now try using your entire vocal trampoline while lying on the floor. Begin with some drain noises. Now give out some basic personal information: name, address, description ('eyes – blue; weight – too much'), where you work, what you think about yourself. Then sing a song. Anywhere in the middle of all this . . . make some more drain noises.

You are less likely to stiffen if you sing or talk while lying on the floor. And, of course, your vocal trampoline works in just the same way when you are standing up.

Some revision

Where is all your speaking and singing equipment?

1 The *voice* is situated in the LARYNX.
2 The *larynx* is suspended from the HYOID BONE.
3 The TONGUE rises out of the *hyoid bone*.
4 The *hyoid bone* is situated in the front of the throat, just under the chin. It is stabilised by a muscle called OMOHYOID ('*omo*' refers to 'shoulder'). This muscle is attached to the *hyoid bone* and to the shoulder blade and passes through a loop at the base of the neck.
5 The SOFT PALATE is the fleshy continuation of the roof of the mouth or *hard palate*. It is flexible enough to make elastic shapes in that part of the throat which is behind and above the mouth. These elastic shapes regulate air pressure in the throat relative to mouth and nose spaces and also assist in articulation of words.
6 The DIAPHRAGM is a dome-shaped muscle inserted under the ribs and effectively dividing the body in half. It is the main breathing muscle and the strongest spring in the human vocal trampoline.
7 The PELVIC FLOOR functions as part of the human vocal trampoline. It responds to the action of the *diaphragm* and the *soft palate* with which it is linked via the nervous system. These three areas must co-ordinate during speaking and singing, and any stiffening of one will bring about a corresponding stiffening in the other two.

Here is a diagram corresponding to the seven points of revision. Label it according to the revision list. Make sure you include all the words printed in capital letters.

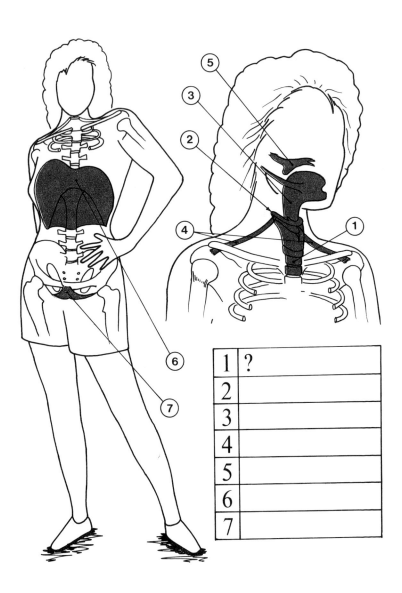

1	?
2	
3	
4	
5	
6	
7	

Do this in pencil first in case you get it wrong and want to start again. You could also use this diagram to label the position of everything else you have learnt so far.

Summary

This Chapter has been concerned with identifying some of the parts of the body concerned with speaking and singing. I have deliberately selected those areas which are not generally associated with the action of the voice and yet have a radical effect on its use when not included in the action or when misused through lack of understanding.

Most voice problems are caused not by inadequacy in the voice itself but by the stiffening of some of these parts. The exercises in Chapter One are specifically designed to bring about a release of that stiffening, thus allowing vocal springs to operate more strongly and efficiently.

Does this mean that from now on every time you go for an interview you have to hit the floor before saying 'Good morning. . . .'? No! It is so that you know the difference between standing STILL and standing STIFF.

Standing STILL can be described as:

YOU, STANDING THERE, ALERT,
BALANCED AND FEELING CONFIDENT

This depends on the condition of the frame within which the voice will speak or sing.

On page 40 are some photographs of common ways of standing, common ways of balancing the frame upon which the spring mechanism of the voice must 'bounce'. Decide which figures could be described as ALERT, BALANCED and CONFIDENT.

Decide which figures would be able to use the voice most easily and efficiently. Perhaps you could imagine that some of the figures *are* talking or singing.

Can you go on to recognise which springs would not operate in some of these figures?

Making time for your exercises

A daily routine of the exercises in this Chapter would be ideal. You haven't time? Here are some ways to cut corners.

Places to do the first exercise on the tape when the frame and springs will generally be working well:

Cleaning your teeth: the tongue works very well singing 'gah' when it is also dealing with a toothbrush. The jaw often opens further than normal to clean the back of the teeth. You can turn away from the mirror and point around the bathroom. Drain noises work well with teeth cleaning.

Up and down stairs: balance is usually improved going up and down stairs. Try walking *backwards* downstairs and singing your 'gah' sounds or a nursery rhyme. The pelvic floor is usually freed in the action of stair climbing. Imagine the plant on your head so that your back remains upright from stair to stair.

You will just have to make time for 'Shakeout' and 'Dead Beetle' exercises, but they are good for shaking out tension and frustration – time well spent.

You may now have a totally different 'feel' about what singing means. So let's sing something. And just to make it easy for you, let's sing it in Russian!

⌨ EXERCISE ❸ *Russian folk song*

This is a Russian folk song. Russian is an exciting language to sing because the arrangement of syllables encourages the use of the back of the tongue, that part that lies in the throat.

What to do

Listen to the tape once to accustom yourself to the sound of the song. You are going to sing each line slowly by following the sounds printed below, following me on the tape. You are also going to hit the floor before each line! Do not worry about getting the sounds correct at this stage. Go for it and allow your brain and voice to sort out the Russian in their own time.

Further work

Try singing the song through slowly while standing on your wobble board.

Russian folk song

RA – STVYE – TA – LEE – YA – BLO – NEE – EE – GROO – SHEE

PO – PLI – LEE – TOO – MA – NI – NA – DRE – KOY.

VWI – HO – DEE – LA – NA – BE – RE – KA – TYOO – SHA,

NA – VWI – SO – KI, NA – BE – RE – KROO – TOY.

(This is how it sounds – the Russian is on page 204.)

2

Out of
Breath

M any people have breathing problems when they try to talk outside the range of their normal conversation. 'Outside normal conversation' would include reciting, taking part in a play, making a speech, having an interview, or even interviewing someone else. Under these circumstances you may find that sentences become shorter because of the need to stop and breathe. There may be an accompanying sensation of tightness in the chest, a feeling that you just cannot breathe quickly enough to take in the required amount of air to say what you have to say. This feeling creates nervousness which increases the tightness in the chest until the whole thing becomes a nightmare and you forget what you are saying. Familiar?

There is a corresponding pattern in singing. You begin by making sure that you have enough breath for the first line. By the time that you are three-quarters through it all that air seems to have been used up and you are drowning. You stop and breathe at the most appropriate place in the line. This divides the line into two 'easy' phrases. Strangely enough, that doesn't appear to make a great deal of difference. You still only just make the end of the short phrase, so the feeling of insecurity remains. It is enough to prevent your ever giving a solo performance in case you run out of breath.

'I get out of breath'

'I am 28 and I have an 18-month-old daughter and a part-time job in a shop selling shoes. I have joined a choir because I have always loved singing, but I'm having problems with my breathing. I feel I haven't got enough breath to sing. I've tried taking a bigger breath to start with, but I think I need to do some breathing exercises to make me breathe deeper. My voice also gets tired at the shop after a long day. My throat aches after work and after choir practice. I feel it is something to do with being "out of breath" all the time.'

'Come for a lesson.'
'Can I bring my little girl?'
'Yes.'

My studio is at the top of a hill and this lady arrives with a bag containing her music and her daughter in a carrybag on her back. She sings me a song and, in spite of elaborate preparation of the way that she stands, and visible expansion of the whole rib cage, she does not even get to the end of the first page without the breathing system showing signs of acute discomfort. By then I too am experiencing discomfort. I wish she would stop and put herself and me out of the agony of it all. This is precisely how the audience reacts to this 'out of breath' situation. Even if you manage the task in hand the audience is dying for you to stop so they can all relax.

But here is a woman carrying a baby on her back up and down escalators, up hills, with no problem. Breathing is totally efficient and therefore totally ignored.

So what is happening?

There are two breathing systems existing here.
System 1: for carrying the child to the lesson.

Characteristics:
a Efficient.
b No conscious control.
c Adjustable – she had sat on the train, walked on the flat, walked up the hill.
d It worked at all times without difficulty. All times, that is, when she was not talking or singing.

System 2: for talking and singing.

Characteristics:
a Totally inefficient.
b Consciously controlled.
c Unable to adjust to different conditions, long phrases, short phrases, loud, soft, and so on.
d Temporary – it had collapsed before the end of the song.

Obviously the second system needs to be phased out. The talking and singing needs the flexibility, strength and automatic reflex of the more efficient system used when carrying the baby on her back.

We must first understand the difference between these two systems and then discover what action or thought brings about the change from one system to another. However, before I explain these two systems, it would be useful for you to consider what you already know or believe about breathing and, in particular, anything that you feel about *your* breathing.

Find a blank sheet of paper and pen or pencil. Instead of writing a list, try drawing a picture of what you feel about your breathing.

Your first picture will probably be awkward if you are used to listing your thoughts, but this system is more fun and stretches your imagination.

When you have reviewed your own ideas about breathing here are two exercises which will help you to experience efficient breathing.

Exercises to observe your breathing

🔲 EXERCISE ❹ *Running on the spot*

What to do

You are going to swing your arms rhythmically, observing what happens to your breathing. Listen to the tape, read the notes that follow and then have a go.

Notes

Before you begin swinging your arms, place one foot in front of the other as if you had taken a step forward. Distribute the weight evenly on both feet, arms hanging at your sides. Imagine you have a plant pot on your head. This will help you to keep your head balanced and in line with your back. Now swing your arms rhythmically as though you were running but do not move your feet. Enjoy the twisting of the rib cage as the arms change position. Finally, allow your knees to bend with each *downswing* of the arms.

This is a useful movement for many voice exercises, so check in the mirror for the following:

- loose, swinging arms not lifting above shoulder height;
- knees which fall away from each other as they bend;
- forward-pointing feet;
- a bottom which follows the line of the back and head.

When you have found a slow, strong swing, breathe OUT through the mouth energetically and noisily to 'HA!' using only your breath to make the sound, no voice. Breathe out noisily on each downswing. Your mouth should remain open throughout and the noisy 'HA!' should feel as if it comes from the back of the throat.

Keep this exercise going for a minute or so at a time, then put the other foot in front and repeat the exercise. Listen to the noisy out-breath.

What do you notice about the space between the noisy out-breaths? Nothing? Good. There should be nothing to notice because when this exercise is well set up – keep checking yourself in the mirror against the illustrations and instructions – the space between out-breaths is silent.

Although you are breathing in at this moment you are breathing in naturally. That is, REFLEXLY, AUTOMATICALLY, SILENTLY, INSTANTLY, FULLY, DEEPLY and WITHOUT EFFORT.

The purpose of the 'running on the spot' exercise is to shift the emphasis from breathing *in* to breathing OUT.

EXERCISE • *Now sing the Russian folk song*

'Run on the spot' and when you experience a strong, slow, swinging rhythm, and after taking two or three strong out-breaths and silent in-breaths, break into the Russian Folk Song.

Here are some points to note:

1 When you have performed a task, breathing in happens automatically to replace the oxygen used by the muscles.
2 Rhythm plays a large part in the efficiency of this process.
3 The twisting of the upper trunk encourages the ribs to move independently of each other and not move as a fixed 'cage', but as a basket.

These points will become clearer as you read and work on.

'Running on the spot' is a very simple but very effective exercise for changing your attitude to your own breathing. Do it regularly; it will help you to understand the replacement system by which all breathing naturally operates.

EXERCISE ❺ *On 'Oi!'*

'Oi!!' This is what you would shout at someone who is making off with your bike as you come out of a shop. It is a spontaneous reaction expressing a mixture of surprise and indignation, an instant response without forethought. 'Oi!'. It is a wonderful voicework sound which you can play with.

What to do

Listen to my 'Oi!'s on the tape, and then compete with me. Then repeat the exercise but hit the floor first before springing up to a standing position, pointing at an object and 'Oi!'ing at it. (Review the hitting the floor and springing up exercise on pages 25–7, first if you need to.)

Further work

Make a little physical investigation of this 'Oi!'. Place one hand on your chest, just below your throat, and one hand across your pubic bone. (Find your pubic bone by covering your pubic hair with the flat of your hand.) You now have one hand at the top and one hand at the bottom of your trunk.

Shout 'Oi!' and observe the reaction in these two areas. Do not breathe in to shout! There isn't a reaction in your pubic area? Then you really didn't care about your bike being stolen and so you are being polite and respectable in order not to be embarrassed. OR you have taken a breath before shouting 'Oi!'. You don't need to do that, so don't do it. Mean it! – from the bottom of your gut! Now you should have the same reaction both ends.

Now 'Oi!' with a plant on your head. Stand in front of the mirror and make quite sure that your head remains still when you shout 'Oi!'.

⌨ EXERCISE ❻ *'Sunday' by Louis McNeice*

This poem by Louis McNeice is printed on page 205.

What to do

I am going to read it on the tape line by line, shouting 'Oi!' at the beginning of each line, and pausing at the end of each line. Listen to me doing it first, read the notes below and then copy me using your own versions of 'Oi!'. When you have become familiar with the technique, finish the poem off for yourself.

Notes

You do not breathe in before the first 'Oi!' 'Oi!' is part of the line – no break between 'Oi!' and the first word.

On the pause, the air will flood into you silently, effortlessly, deeply, rapidly, instantly – leave your mouth open so that it can. Remember, breathe only in the pauses, not between 'Oi!' and the line.

Here are the first four lines of the poem, which are on the tape:

OI! Down the road someone is practising scales (Pause)
OI! The notes like little fishes vanish with a wink of tails (Pause)
OI! Man's heart expands to tinker with his car (Pause)
OI! For this is Sunday morning, Fate's great bazaar

Don't forget to perform the rest of the poem in the same way for yourself. It's on page 205.

Further work

You may use this exercise on other poems but the rhythm of poetry is necessary if this exercise is to work well. It is also useful to use the same exercise while singing.

We are naturally endowed with two different systems of breathing. One is the system by which my pupil walked up the hill with the baby on her back. The other is an emergency system which, unfortunately, she was using for talking and singing.

The first system my pupil used is the one you have been using for the last two exercises. Call it the 'Activity System'. The second system we will call the 'Emergency System'. Let's look at the Activity System first.

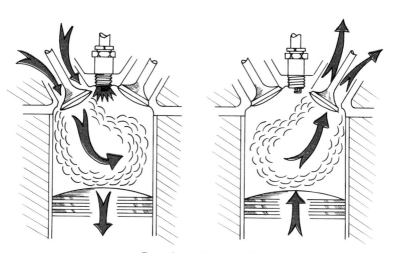

Breathing In And Out

Activity system

You are aware that breathing consists of breathing in and breathing out. In the activity system you have an automatic reflex in the brain which makes you breathe IN. Every few seconds, regardless of your desire to prevent it, a nerve impulse from the brain 'fires'. The message is sent to the diaphragm to contract and its dome shape flattens, thus allowing more space for the lungs. Physical law states that air moves from a high pressure to a low pressure, so air is drawn into the low pressure in the lungs, (created by the flattening diaphragm), from the higher pressure all around you.

EXERCISE • *Experiment*

Breathe out and decide never to breathe again. Wait –
and see what happens. Are you still there? Of course
you are. At some point the nerve fired in your head
and you breathed in, in spite of your conscious control.

When enough oxygen is provided for activity the
firing automatically stops and the contraction releases,
returning the diaphragm back to its natural dome
shape. The lungs are compressed by this return to
shape and the air in them achieves a higher pressure
than the air outside. Air is drawn out to even the
pressure. Different activities trigger different
breathing patterns. For example, sitting in a chair,
reading, promotes quite shallow breathing with a
'firing of the diaphragm muscle about every three
seconds.

EXERCISE • *The waiting game*

Sit easily in a chair and visualise your breathing as a
process of firing and letting go. When your attention
becomes really centred on your breathing, play a game
of *waiting* for the mechanism to fire.

1	Breathe out	**2**	Wait for automatic firing
3	Breathe out	**4**	Wait for automatic firing

and so on. Continue the game for several minutes.

If breathing in is an automatic reflex it is vital that it
is allowed to function undisturbed.

When you are sitting quietly – reading, sunbathing,
sleeping – your breathing will imperceptibly tick over
on the system I have described. Now you wish to go

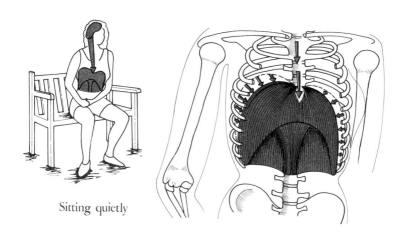

Sitting quietly

into more energetic activity. What happens to the breathing system then? You want to run, skip, dance, sing, talk. How is this extra energy, this extra oxygen, drawn into the system? These activities obviously necessitate a more expansive system, deeper breathing, more movement of air.

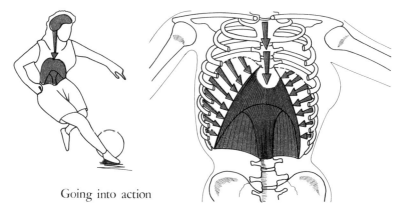

Going into action

You are sitting in your deckchair reading while the kids play football on the beach. Then they begin to quarrel and it becomes necessary for you to join the game to keep the peace. Reluctantly you get up, walk down the beach and begin to kick the ball about.

You have just made all kinds of different movements in a variety of speeds. These movements and speed changes require the work of many different muscle patterns. Simply, you used your back, buttocks, arms, legs, feet, probably voice as well.

The various muscle systems contracted and relaxed in a rhythmic pattern. As they did so the firing mechanism in the brain adapted to the standing up, then changed its firing for the amble down the beach. Another gear for the running, yet another, perhaps only for a moment, for the quick side step as your son tries to trip you up during the football game.

This breathing system can be compared to a car with an automatic gearbox. As you change speed or the engine works harder on hills the gears automatically move up or down to provide the necessary fuel for the job. The body has thousands of these gears. They are breathing rhythm patterns.

As you run for the ball the stretch required in the back will use energy – the action of the diaphragm will intensify to replace it.

This is a change of breathing rhythm:

As you kick the ball the power in the goal you score will be replaced by the firing of a long, deep breath.

Another automatic change:

When you have kicked the ball and you stop running.

Another gear change in the breath.

How and why do we interfere with this automatic

system and create inefficient breathing? What do we do that is so terrible? We take a breath. But surely that is the same as breathing in?

No, taking a breath is something quite different from the automatic impulse which fires our breathing. Taking a breath is *you* deciding when to breathe and how much breath you need. It is about you controlling the system. By taking a quick breath you change an automatic system into a manual system.

Because the motorcar figures so prominently in our lives, I often use it to explain voices. For those who drive an automatic car, taking a breath is like 'kick-down' which you use to over-ride the system of automatic gear change in order to overtake. You stamp on the accelerator, which has the effect of dropping to a much lower gear by suddenly racing the engine. The car leaps forward. However, this should only be for sudden emergency overtaking. To use it too frequently would damage your engine.

Go back to the exercise 'Experiment' on page 52. First repeat this 'No More Breathing' test: breathe out, wait and do not breathe again until the firing occurs. Try this several times (with rests in between) observing which parts of you are activated. Do you feel sensations in your diaphragm only? Or are there other places which join in at the end of that very long wait? where are these other places?

> Your back?
> Abdomen?
> Legs?
> Chest?

After this experiment, try a new one. Breathe out, count to four, and then breathe in on your own decision. Does that feel at all different? What is different this time? Does your body behave differently? How do your back, abdomen, legs, chest, behave this time?

Take time to play around with both these experiments. Two minutes of allowed firing, two minutes of deciding to breathe. When you *decide* to breathe in rather than allowing for the reflex to fire you immediately engage System II, which is:

The Emergency System of breathing

Suppose you are standing on a street corner, not using much energy, and a man comes at you with a knife. You have two choices – run or fight. Either way you have to create great energy instantly, but your firing mechanism will need a message from the muscles. You see the problem and you need to override normal energy levels in order to create emergency power/ strength/speed/noise, and so on. You need to contact your emergency system and you achieve this by taking a short, sharp noisy breath when you see the problem before you.

This short, sharp breath interrupts the normal rhythm of breathing. It is the switch which activates your survival system. Having activated it you are in shock. The depth of shock is relative to the emergency which you have to face. Whatever the emergency, however, be it the challenge of some silly lie you have told or aquaplaning on the motorway, the switch is always the same – TAKE A QUICK BREATH. When that switch is thrown there is an immediate increase in the

adrenalin level, your heartbeat, the speed of your
breathing (but not necessarily its depth) and your
energy level. You 'puff up'. In this condition you may
well not only face your attacker but kill him. I
exaggerate. However, the system does cater for those
occasions when you need more strength, courage,
daring, than you believe you possess.

This system of taking a quick breath to stiffen
yourself for an emergency task engages 'Startle
Pattern'. Startle pattern can be recognised by a quicker
beating of the heart, the pulsing of the blood in the
ears, quicker, noisier breathing and a feeling of
excitement. Is this familiar? Where have you
experienced it? Maybe at the dentist, at an interview,
waiting to sing a song, before an examination. We
often refer to it as 'nerves'.

Take a breather

Maybe it is time to take not a breath but a breather. Put
the book away for a week. You have, after all, come a
long way if you have done everything so far *and* played
the tape on your way to work. So that you will not
completely lose touch here are some observations to
make during your week's rest.

Do you take a breath before you:

Unscrew a rather tight top on a jar?
Pull a cork out of a bottle?
Lift a weight off the floor?
Reach for something on a high shelf?
Move from sitting to standing?
Speak? Sing?

If you do, stop it – these are not emergencies.

Take the week to adjust your thinking about breathing.

If you never interrupt your natural breathing system which automatically breathes for you, you will only use your emergency system for *real* emergencies. You do not need to concern yourself with whether you will recognise, and thus be ready for, the emergency, should it happen. Your first motivation is to survive. Keep refusing to 'take a breath' and you will not be drawn into false situations of emergency. For example:

The letter about your overdraft
Your son's punk haircut
Your daughter's boyfriend
Singing a solo at the local Music Festival
Answering the telephone
Standing up to a bully
Missing the 8:15.
Stuck in traffic.

These are not emergencies – so do not take a sudden breath at the outset. This will upset your breathing, maybe all day. When we stop taking a breath at these moments we may discover the *real* emergencies and thus the appropriate breathing system will always be engaged.

EXERCISE ❼ *'How doth the little crocodile'*

What to do

I am going to read the poem out on the tape while standing on a wobble board and balancing a

This poem is printed on page 205 at the end of the book.

plant on my head. Listen to my performance first, then follow me line by line using your own wobble board and plant if you are in a suitable place!

Notes

Observe whether you can repeat what I say without 'taking a breath' before you begin.

Further work

Choose another poem which has large print and short lines. (I am aware that this is not a sensitive approach to the choice of poetry, but right now I am dealing with the efficiency of the breathing and maintaining that during the activity of speech.) Place the book open on a stand and put your plant on your head.

Stand for a moment observing how your breathing 'fires'. You are to say the first line when you can do it without taking a breath and without altering your breathing rhythm in any way. Merely look at the first line, mentally hear it, then – go for it. At the end of the line you wait for the opportunity to say the next line. That opportunity will occur after the automatic reflex has replaced what you have used in saying the first line. You will have little success with this at first. Do not care about that. Keep sending the messages. Be patient – have a sense of humour. Persevere gently: after all, you do look quite ridiculous reading poetry with a plant on your head – so . . . smile while you do it. Put the plant down, massage your face, start again.

Why interfere?

Why do we interfere with the natural system of breathing so much in talking and singing?

Poor or misguided instruction. I began by describing a lesson. During that lesson I noticed that when I played the introduction to a song the pupil waited and then, before she began singing, she took a breath. I asked her why she did this. 'I was told.' 'Who told you?' She had to think very hard and then she came to the conclusion that it was the sum total of lots of 'hints' on how the voice operated. Examples:

- In the school choir she had frequently been told to take a deep breath for long phrases.
- Conductors, she remembered, frequently threw back their heads and took a breath to show the moment of entry for the choir.
- A singing teacher had given her breathing exercises requiring her to breathe in or out to the count of whatever.
- She had been told to support her voice 'on the breath'. As she didn't understand this but didn't like to say so she worked it out for herself thus

Support – means strength – means control – means tension.

Where can I get that tension from? I will tense my diaphragm because that feels like control which feels like strength which feels like support, control it myself.

This is how you consciously control the diaphragm. Try it. Take a quick breath. You can get hold of the diaphragm from inside.

By trial and error she discovered that if she took a breath the energy produced could sustain all the demands of her singing teacher or her choir practice or her rehearsal or her Manager at the shoe shop for the length of time required. The fact that she collapsed entirely after these sessions indicated to her that she must have given of her best.

When we are at work, the sudden tense moments of the day can promote the same response.

'Have you done that Report?'
'I must see you about this month's figures!'

You had forgotten. A quick intake of breath, followed by a defensive answer side-steps the problem. This tense, 'bottled' energy could be what you operate on all the time. Some people take a sudden breath as they open the office door in the morning, open the car door before a long journey, unlock their business, thus changing their whole day into a state of emergency. The voice is then imperious, unnaturally pushy or overpowering. This bubble will burst sooner or later. It usually occurs when the day is finally over. The intense weariness which comes after such tension may then produce 'inert before the television' for the evening or 'tired all weekend'.

If you review Chapter One, The Human Vocal Trampoline, you will see that the natural spring in the system, when activated, creates even more spring not collapse and exhaustion. Taking a breath interrupts anything that you are doing. Breathing is automatic – you do not have to do it for it to happen both easily and efficiently. Check yourself in the mirror. Say a line of poetry without taking a breath to do it. Allow yourself to breathe at the *end* of the first phrase. Observe how much more at ease the body is when you do not blow yourself up like a balloon to begin, how much more easily and silently you go on breathing after saying the line.

Taking a breath, that is, *deciding* when we breathe in, engages the emergency system, tightening the throat and, in consequence, making the whole trampoline system rigid. The voice, then, does not work efficiently or reliably. Neither does the rest of you.

Talking and Eating

EXERCISE • *Observing your jaw*

You will need an apple, a carrot, or something equally crunchy, and a glass of water.

We are so familiar, or so we believe, with the mouth, tongue and throat area that we take for granted the way

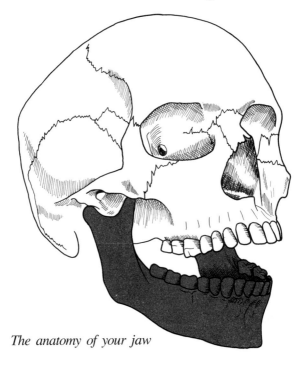

The anatomy of your jaw

the various parts work together. So . . . first, discover your jaw.

Notice where the jaw joins the skull. Find the place by poking around your cheeks just in front of your ear. If you move your jaw from side to side location is easier. With your fingers on that joint look in the mirror and move your jaw around through all its possibilities. Notice the effect of these different movements on your face and on the position of your head on your neck.

Have your apple and glass handy, sit in front of the mirror and observe your jaw movement:

1 from the front – with your eyes;
2 from the side – with your fingers on the joint.

Check yourself against the photographs on the next page.

Select one of the following words to describe the degree of **activity in your jaw** as you perform the following movements:

	NONE?	SOME?	STRONG ACTIVITY?
1 Chew and swallow some of your apple	☐	☐	☐
2 Drink the water	☐	☐	☐
3 Talk to yourself (keep watching)	☐	☐	☐
4 Sing (keep watching)	☐	☐	☐

All these activities fall into two different categories: you are either taking something *in* or putting something *out* of your mouth.

Freedom and mobility

Jaw braced against skull

A big mouthful coming

Maximum space in the throat

YOU PUT IN	YOU PUT OUT
Food	Talking
Drink	Singing
Air	Air

Let us examine each action separately. What are the demands for:

Putting In – eating and drinking?

1   A wide open mouth at the chin end and space in the mouth to move food about: achieved by opening and closing the teeth.
2   Strength in the jaw to use the surfaces of the teeth for cutting and grinding, the jaw braced against the skull.
3   The soft palate helps to close the space at the back of the mouth until swallowing is required (you don't want food to slip down the throat accidentally).
4   The tongue moves relative to the cutting and grinding action of the jaw, so that it does not get bitten and can move food onto the cutting surfaces.

and Putting Out – talking and singing?

1   The maximum space at the back of the mouth and in the whole length of the throat extending upwards behind the nose and downwards to the

level of the shoulders. This ensures space for maximum spring in the soft palate and tongue.

2   No cutting or grinding, so no *strength* required of the jaw, but maximum *flexibility*.

3   No particularly large space required at front of mouth, just freedom and mobility.

4   The tongue, as the main articulator needs to move anywhere. As jaw and tongue are attached, there is no way they can move completely independently but in talking and singing the tongue must move and the jaw must follow.

As you can easily see the two activities are not only different, they are actually making quite opposite demands. The two activities are therefore controlled by quite different sets of muscles. Only by changing the action of the jaw according to whether you are talking or eating will you achieve maximum efficiency with minimum effort.

I shall call the 'Putting In' or eating action:

the CONTROLLED JAW

and the 'Putting Out' or talking action:

the FREE JAW

Before going on to investigate the muscles which activate these two jaw positions, it is time to approach the information practically.

Pinning up your face

Look at the left-hand photograph on page 67. With the index fingers of each hand Pat is picking up her upper lip and 'pinning' it to the cheekbone alongside her nostril. This exposes the upper teeth across the

Your fingers need to direct up and away from each other. Elbows out to the side

Lifting one cheek away from the upper teeth. Pull up and out

front of the mouth and spreads quite a large area of the face sideways. Look at your face in the mirror. Pick up your face with your fingers, pin it up and note the difference. Release it and give your face a really good massage. Now repeat the 'pin up' and you are ready to begin.

EXERCISE ❽ *Reading a recipe*

What to do

First, listen to this exercise on the tape, and while you listen keep lifting and releasing your face to encourage muscles in your upper lip and at the sides of your nostrils to wake up.

Now pin up your face and keeping it pinned up read through the recipe directions

Poooooooooooooor

The water and lemon juice over the raisins and

Leeeeeeeeeeeeeeeeeeve

to soak while preparing the fruit.

Cooore and Sliiiice the apples,

Sliiiiiice the bananas, diviiiide

the orange into segments and Seeeeee eeeeeeeeeeeeeeee the grapes. Miiiiix with the raisins.

Puuuut the muesli base into a bowl, Poooor

on the fruit, Aaaadd the nuts and Miiii

iiiiiix well. Suuuuuuuuuuuuuu with fruit juice.

below without the tape. You may experience some difficulty with the 'p' of 'pour' and 'preparing'. Allow the lower lip to move towards the upper lip for this sound instead of the normal pattern of the other way round. This allows a release in the upper lip which should make it all much easier.

Recipe:

Pour the water and lemon juice over the raisins and leave to soak while preparing the fruit. Core and slice the apples, slice the bananas, divide the oranges into segments and seed the grapes. Mix with the raisins. Pour the muesli base into a bowl, pour on the fruit, add the nuts and stir well. Serve with fruit juice.

After a rest, listen to the tape again and then attempt to read and sing with me. You sing each verb on two or three different pitches before going on to read the rest of the sentence. Aim for continuity between singing and speaking. Opposite there is a specially designed version of the recipe to help you.

Notes

When you pin up your face, check with the photographs that you have got it right. After reading, or reading and singing, allow your face to return to normal and give it a good massage. It will probably be quite pink where you have pinned it up. That is good; it will improve circulation and wake up the muscles.

Do not compromise. If there is a tremendous pull down against the pinning up of your face do not allow it. After all, these are only face muscles, so you can win. You are not doing any damage at all by being insistent. Your face has merely become stiff.

Remember to begin without taking a breath and also that it is the flesh on your face which you wish to push up, not the bone of the skull. The skull should remain balanced on your neck – eyes looking forward. Check with your mirror.

Further work

As you become accustomed to swapping from singing to talking become bolder in your singing of the verb, but keep that face well and truly pinned up.

After you have had a really good go at all this and your face feels thoroughly pink, give the exercise one last, pinned up, great big sing/talk. Now let your face go and READ the recipe normally, observing any differences.

So, what did you notice about pinning up your face to speak and sing? Are you surprised that it is not difficult to articulate words with your face in that position? Perhaps it is easier.

Has your voice changed at all during this exercise? Has it become richer or dropped in pitch. Does your articulation (ability to pronounce words) feel freer? Easier? Smoother?

I believe that all these qualities will have emerged in this last reading. Why am I so sure? You have been talking with a free jaw and not with a jaw in the position of biting and chewing. If you habitually talk with your jaw in the chewing, biting position, you will limit the pitch and dynamics of your voice. An over strong jaw prevents 'spring' in the vocal trampoline. If you can learn to talk and sing with a free jaw you make it possible to realise your vocal potential.

Now you have had a chance to experience talking and singing with a free jaw, back to your apple, carrot and drink of water (page 63). Feel how much 'longer' your face becomes to eat and drink, the cheeks flattening against the teeth and the jaw crunching. Put your hand again on your jaw joint and feel the strength of the bite. While you are chewing, pin your face up again. Keep your lips together (otherwise wear a bib!). You will find that even with your lips together you can no longer control the food in your mouth. The tongue ceases to do its proper job.

Now you have experienced both actions of the jaw,

here are two diagrams showing the different muscles which bring about these two actions and where they are located. You can then choose to live with a free jaw using a controlled jaw only to eat and drink.

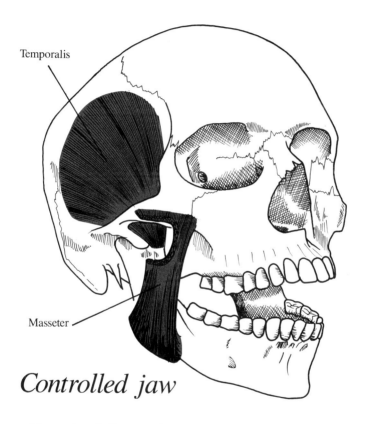

Temporalis

Masseter

Controlled jaw

Note the following muscles in your controlled jaw:

Temporalis is your snapping muscle. Place your hands on either side of your head and snap your teeth together.

Masseter This holds the jaw shut after it has been 'snapped'. It will hold the jaw in any position from wide open to closed and is the strongest muscle in your body for its size. (This is the one you would use to swing from a trapeze by your teeth.) Place your hand on your jaw and clench your teeth to feel this.

Go back to your list of observations and check for strong activity to discover how much biting and chewing you are doing when you are *not* actually eating. Does your list record strong activity in talking and singing? This indicates that you are using the same jaw action for talking and singing as you are for chewing and biting. That is not unusual. Most people use their jaws in this way. But it is not very efficient and

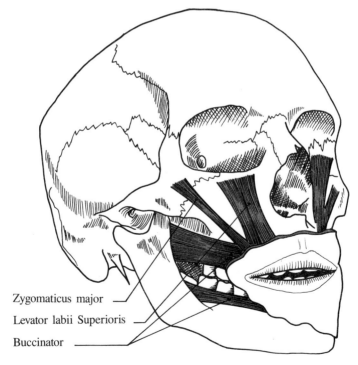

Zygomaticus major ——

Levator labii Superioris ——

Buccinator ——

Free jaw

requires tremendous effort. The big eating and snapping muscles are designed to operate in short, strong bursts, not in long, continuous periods of activity. We must limit these muscles to the job for which they were designed.

Note the following muscles in your free jaw:

Zygomaticus Major and Minor　These are called the laughing muscles because that is their main use. Maybe that is why we associate singing with happiness.

Buccinator　The trumpet muscle so called because it needs to be strengthened to play one. It forms the lower cheek.

Levator labii superioris　The Latin for 'lifter of the upper lip'. This muscle fans the upper lip upwards and outwards assisting the other two muscles in 'opening' the face outwards from the side of the nose.

Look at the directions of the muscles in the two diagrams discussed above. Can you see that the muscles which free the jaw generally oppose the direction of masseter? That the muscles which control the jaw operate vertically? The muscles which free the jaw operate laterally or are fan shaped for flexibility. There is more choice of movement here.

More choice . . . More freedom . . .

Think of this whenever you speak and also watch the faces of people speaking to you. When the jaw is free the face is more active around the area of the eyes and the upper cheeks. The face appears to widen for speech and singing. If the jaw is not free the face remains stiff and rather expressionless when talking or singing. Often, through years of strong jaw movement, heavy muscle develops on the jaw line.

Can you understand now why pinning up the face alongside the nostril gives you so much freedom of articulation? You are stimulating that area where the muscles of a free jaw insert into the front of the skull, thus encouraging them to operate. This gives priority for tongue movement. If the jaw is not free, the message from brain to tongue is: 'We are eating. Get in line!'

In many people, this is a very 'dead' area of the face. We even have a phrase for it in the United Kingdom – 'the stiff upper lip'. It comes alive when you smile, laugh, or clean your teeth, but these muscles need to be permanently active if your jaw is to remain free and your face lively and expressive.

⌨ EXERCISE ❾ *Taking a handful of face*

Here is another exercise to give you an experience of the release of masseter and a spacious experience of talking.

What to do

Take hold of one cheek – a good handful – and lift the whole cheek up and away from your upper teeth. Hold it there for a moment or two and then let go. With the other hand repeat this on the other side of your face. Check what you are doing using the photograph on page 67. Repeat each side several times to give your face a good stretch.

You are going to repeat short pieces of poetry after me on the tape with one cheek lifted away from your upper teeth all the time. Change sides every two lines. You can go straight into this exercise without listening to the whole of it on the tape first. The poems are printed on pages 205–206.

Notes

Begin the lifting movement before you begin the line of

poetry, and then change sides every two lines.

Further work

Repeat the exercise, either singing the poem on tape to your own tune, or using a poem and tune of your own. Remember to begin without taking a breath.

One of the very best exercises for linking talking and singing to freeing the jaw is . . .

EXERCISE • *Be a ventriloquist*

Even a bad attempt at being a ventriloquist is a very good exercise. The idea is to make your tongue and soft palate do the whole job of talking, not allowing your face muscles and lips to help. Adopt a fairly open mouth and excessive 'widening' of the face (using all those 'sideways' muscles) and away you go. A toothbrush cleaning your back upper teeth helps. It may sound peculiar, but when you repeat the poem normally afterwards the sensation of talking is wonderful.

At the beginning of this chapter you were asked to observe your own jaw during activities performed by the mouth and throat. Try these activities again (on page 63), but this time push up the sides of your upper lip against your cheekbones as you did in Exercise 8. You will not be able to eat or drink with your face in this position. You have already discovered why. All the other activities are not only possible but much less effort when the jaw is free. The jaw moves less and the mouth and throat gain more space and freedom to perform their various tasks. This is your jaw position for everything except biting, chewing and drinking.

The biting, chewing muscles of masseter and temporalis are grossly overworked in most people. You can prove this quite easily for yourself by spending just one day observing the faces of everyone around you. As you have seen, masseter is a muscle running vertically on the sides of the face. Overworking this muscle produces a rather dead and expressionless face with most weight in the jawline. Only eating seems to bring this stiff face to life, because talking and eating are on the same system. Exercising one increases the chances of the other occurring. If you want to talk to the man who has sat opposite to you on the train for the last two years, saying nothing, offer him a sandwich. As he contracts and relaxes these two big muscles to bite and chew you may also be able to prise a few words out of him as the suspensory mechanism – the vocal trampoline – and the larynx receive some stimulus from the space created now and again by swallowing.

The masseter and temporalis muscles can be released at all times when you are not eating and drinking. YOU CAN *LIVE* WITH A FREE JAW, CLOSING THE SPACE BETWEEN JAW AND SKULL ONLY TO EAT.

Advantages of living with a free jaw

1 Breathing

Poke about on your face until you find the edge of your cheekbone just below your eye. With the other hand locate your collarbone. Between your hands is the approximate length of your throat – your *pharynx*. The whole of this tube, including the passage out through the nose and the passage out through the mouth, becomes constricted in its middle section, the *oropharynx* ('oro' meaning 'mouth'), by the contraction of masseter and the holding of the jaw. Breathing is a reflex and when the diaphragm contracts air comes into the throat, silently moving from the high pressure outside you to a low pressure inside you. If the throat tube narrows halfway down, however, air will be sucked past that narrow part by the more expanded lower throat. This creates noisy breathing – you can *hear* the sucking. When you run or sing or play tennis the breathing becomes even noisier. Fit, active people should not have noisy breathing. When the throat is not narrowed in this central section because the jaw is free and masseter relaxed, breathing immediately becomes more efficient and quieter.

2 Overload

Dentists generally agree that tightening of the jaw, for which masseter is largely responsible, is the cause of some of the nerve pain which we may describe as toothache. I have worked with many people to change their use of the jaw because it was interfering with their articulation or limiting their singing potential. Many of them have subsequently admitted that, having lived for a while with a free jaw, headaches previously associated with pressure of work had disappeared. In some cases these headaches were severe enough to be diagnosed as migraine (See Chapter Four 'Michael' on page 82).

3 Articulation – saying the words

When the jaw is free there is greater freedom of movement for the tongue. The tongue is the main articulator of our language. Two-thirds of the tongue forms the front wall of the throat – the pharynx. This large area of the tongue remains inactive when the jaw is not free. Similarly, the soft palate has little freedom to operate, so the jaw has to 'chew' even more to help to produce the words we want to say. One of the first differences you notice about 'pinning up' the face is the ease with which you can talk when masseter is relaxed. This applies also to the singing of words.

4 Quality and range of the voice

The voice produces its best sound when the throat is expanded for its maximum length. When the throat is in this expanded condition the soft palate can dome and stretch in the upper part of the throat behind the nose – the *nasopharynx*. The throat is lined with muscles. These, and the muscles of the soft palate, assist the tongue in articulation, the pronouncing of words. Restriction in the throat caused by the permanent holding of the jaw by the masseter muscle also restricts this good, easy system of articulation. Talking becomes an effort and sore throats can result because a restricted throat can become inflamed with overwork. A sensation of space in the throat and freedom in the jaw, however, stimulate the whole voice system. As the throat expands, the soft palate and tongue take on a stronger muscular action. The whole front of the face is stimulated by this; it becomes more lively and expressive. The eyes open and widen. The spring in tongue and soft palate is conveyed to the diaphragm and pelvic floor as part of the vocal trampoline. The breathing system then expands to cater for the greater spring in the whole body. This, in turn, floods the brain with oxygen, creating a feeling of vitality and wellbeing. As in a good game of tennis, the more you play the more energy you create and the better you feel.

5   Listening

Elevation of the soft palate stretches the nasopharynx (the back of the nose), opening a tube which connects the throat with the ear, the eustachian tube. When this tube is open sound is going directly from the throat into the ear. I believe this internal listening system to be a contributory factor to singing in tune.

6   Health

I am interested in the steady increase in middle ear infection in children. This seems to have increased at the same time as the decrease in the number of children who sing. I wonder how many of those who suffer from this complaint sing regularly and with a free jaw? Singing with a free jaw exercises the whole ear mechanism from within. Many non-singers have sinus problems which seem to disappear when they learn to sing and to sing with a free jaw. The advantages resulting from learning to live with a free jaw seem endless, and I believe that there are many more – like the ear infection – to be considered and thoroughly researched. Indeed, I could go on to mention balance and posture and even constriction in the lower spine besides voice problems like stammering.

How to live with a free jaw

You can now see that the jaw is an important area to understand and explore. How do you recognise that your jaw is free without pinning up your face? How do you learn to maintain a free jaw at all times except when eating and drinking? There is nothing technical, complicated or difficult about it. You merely have to stimulate the lateral muscles of your face and strengthen them sufficiently so that they work continuously, releasing the masseter muscle at all times except for eating and drinking. There are many small muscles located laterally on your face and others underneath your cheekbone. The load would be spread so that, with ever-changing facial expressions, the jaw could be 'suspended' by a web of small attachments. This is what creates the freedom in the jaw.

Every time you smile . . . your face moves laterally, masseter releases.
SMILE MORE
Every time you laugh . . . your face moves laterally.
LAUGH MORE

There are two very good ways of freeing your jaw.

One is to massage the face in the direction you want it to go, thus waking up the muscles and breaking down the 'toughness' created in the tissue by holding it fixed for so long. The other is to be a ventriloquist when you clean your teeth: say a poem while brushing your back teeth – or sing a song. Be a ventriloquist every time you wash your hands: there is usually a mirror over the basin.

Do not worry about the reaction to your talking to yourself. If you become sufficiently successful at being a ventriloquist no-one will know anyway! Once you have changed to living with a free jaw the muscles which you have stimulated will be operating automatically all the time. You are then home and dry – back to sanity as you clean your teeth.

I hope I have stressed the importance of getting in touch with and, if necessary, changing the use of your jaw. Tightlipped, straightfaced, longfaced, deadpan, pinched: these are all words used to describe what is simply just an overworked masseter muscle.

4

Michael

Michael was not a professional singer although, with his voice, he could have been. A singing career is a precarious one so by becoming an engineer and singing locally Michael enjoyed both security and singing and supplemented his income too.

He was athletic, playing football for a good local club. Everything seemed to come very easily to him. He could work Saturday morning, play football in the afternoon and go on to sing in a concert in the evening. He gardened, replumbed and rewired his house, took A-level English; he was generally versatile and fit. He did, however, feel at a disadvantage with his music, not having had music lessons. He learned his songs by ear or with help from friends. He decided to have some singing lessons.

He was taught to control his breathing, something he had previously never considered, and advised to project everything he sang into the front of his face. He practiced diction exercises and concentrated on holding his ribs out. He tightened his buttocks – 'Imagine you have a bus ticket between them' – and stiffened his legs. As Michael was both fit and well co-ordinated he could change the way he sang quite easily. He could also execute all the controlling tensions very strongly because he was a strong man. He practised so hard and strengthened himself so much that in the next six months the voice had twice the carrying power and several notes on top of his pitch range. He imagined he must be doing the right things. He began to sing higher tenor roles and he realised that he only had to stiffen his legs and tighten his diaphragm in order to drown all the chorus. Very impressive. He acquired a local reputation as a good tenor – there are so few – and, for about five years, his singing was very successful. Then the tension began to narrow his back and the performances became exhausting. The voice cracked on the top notes sometimes and began to slide off pitch. He could correct this by planting his legs more firmly on to the stage but he became stiff as an actor, and when he moved, the pitch slid.

I heard him about ten years ago in an amateur operatic concert. It was excruciating to sit in the audience and listen to what appeared to be someone in intense pain. We joke about terrible singing but I realised many years ago that for a voice to be making really *terrible* noises under extreme tension that voice must be a really good instrument. Otherwise it would merely pack up altogether.

What I heard in that concert was a very good instrument, out of condition and rebelling against lack of freedom and mobility. If the voice had not been so good and singing had not meant so much, Michael would have taken up something else. Who wants to keep putting himself through that?

I rang Michael and asked if he were interested in doing some work with me. He would have tried anything, gone to any lengths to sing again, such is the desperation of someone who has sung well and lost it. The task was to allow him to sing in the same way that he played football or ran or dug in the garden. His earlier singing lessons had separated his singing from the real strength of his back, giving his voice the action of a bicycle pump. His vocal cords had become rigid and lost their connection with sensitivity and emotion.

Michael has worked on and off for ten years to enjoy his singing again. The heartache and pain which he has suffered (both physical and emotional) is difficult to imagine. What most people do when they suffer is to crawl into a secluded place to lick their wounds. When you sing as a soloist and your singing deteriorates, you will suffer humiliation on a public stage with an audience for it. Morover, as Michael remained living in the same area where everyone had heard him deteriorate, it was doubly difficult to begin again.

Michael is currently singing the male lead in the local production of 'Annie Get Your Gun'. He does not sing out of tune and, according to his wife, he is so much happier. I have not seen him for some months but he takes care of his own voice now. There are other changes apart from that of restored self-esteem. When his voice was under tension he suffered very severe migraine: that has gone. He admitted to being difficult to live with. The tension which has gone out of his voice has gone out of his life.

The lesson to be learned from this is to be very careful about voice lessons. Be as careful about your voice as you would be about selecting your children's school, your house insurance or your car. Your voice is an intimate emotional, vulnerable, part of you. Unlike the car it is irreplaceable and you do not have a long enough life to spend ten years putting right the damage done by someone who means well but is incompetent. This may sound extreme but we do tend to take our natural human endowments for granted until they fail us.

It is reasonably easy to become a singing teacher. There is not much information about voices available to the general public, so a musician who sings is assumed to know about singing. If you play the piano and read music you are immediately in a position to teach songs. However, teaching songs is not the same as teaching singing. No-one wants, as in Michael's case, twelve years recovery from bad teaching.

Here is a rough but fairly good guide for sorting out good and bad voice teachers.

- You should be able to move about quite easily when singing, bend down to pick something up off the floor, pour out a glass of water. If your singing instruction limits your movement and interferes with your co-ordination in any way, think about it very carefully.
- Ask questions. Whenever you are given something to do, ask why – 'What is it for?' A good test is always 'Show me'.

If someone services your washing machine and is incompetent you may have to replace it at enormous cost. However, that cost does have a ceiling and you can throw away the machine and use the laundrette. Bad voice teaching does not, unfortunately, just interfere with your voice. It can interfere with your health, your relationships and your self-esteem. Where do you obtain a replacement?

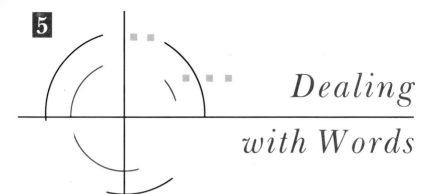

5

Dealing
with Words

I have never worked with a voice, however articulate or expressive, free and flexible, which had not at some time experienced some speech difficulties. We are all likely to stammer when faced with the irate neighbour whose new patio has just been defaced by our dog. Memory and recall do not co-ordinate well in the voice which has to present the all-important marketing plan when the wife is having a baby. The best actors occasionally pace themselves too fast and the most famous voices have 'off' days.

It is only when a speech problem begins to repeat itself regularly that we look for help.

But no-one can assume that their voice will remain in good order through a lifetime of continuous use and pressure without any thought or maintenance. You service your car on a regular basis so that it does not break down, so obviously maintenance is also needed on your voice, which has to work much harder than a car.

How do you pronounce...?

We are beginning to speak at about two years old; by the time children begin school at five they usually speak freely and may well be reading. And it is in *reading* the sounds of speech that one of the conflicts may occur which prevents the best and most natural development of the spoken language. Suppose you were helping a four-year-old read her book and she came to a word she could not pronounce. What would you do to show her how to say it? Look at yourself in the mirror. You are demonstrating how to pronounce the word 'moon'. You want to show how it is said emphasising the sounds of the written letters. Watch yourself find a way to do this.

Did you exaggerate the facial movements you believe are required in order to demonstrate saying the word 'moon'? I bet you did.

We all do this when explaining sounds. We make exaggerated movements with our faces because we believe it gives the pupil a stronger message.

Voluntary and involuntary speech muscles

Your 'voluntary' speech muscles are those muscles which we consciously control. If I tell you to push out your lips, or wrinkle your nose, you can explain to me what you do in order to make these movements. If, on the other hand, you decide to move last night's prawn vindaloo on a bit because it is giving you indigestion, there is nothing you can do to bring that about. Your whole gut, from mouth to anal sphincter, operates on an 'involuntary' basis. You can affect it, but not control it. Your involuntary speech muscles are governed by this rule.

When you demonstrated the pronunciation of 'moon' you used largely *voluntary* muscle to help you. Turn back to page 72 and look at the diagram of the muscles which activate the freeing of the jaw. Look in the mirror and give your face a massage in the area where these muscles originate. It is the small space between the corner of your nose and the corner of your mouth. The bone you can feel protruding above this area is the arch of bone which houses your jaw. Work your fingers across this bone towards your ear and you will arrive at the joint where skull and jaw meet. You have just been examining the most mobile part of your face. Now do some face pulling in front of the mirror, using the photographs as inspiration. Discover how the voluntary muscles in this part of your face contort and twist nose, mouth and cheeks. Do you remember how your face was moved by these muscles as you demonstrated how to say 'moon'?

What about the involuntary speech muscles then? How do they work and how can you affect them? Your whole gut, including mouth and throat, contains strong involuntary muscle. The larynx is suspended within the throat space amid a web of involuntary muscle. You affect involuntary muscle by the whole state of your being: whether you are happy or depressed, nervous or excited. 'I've got a stomach ache', translation: my involuntary stomach muscle is tense with the desire not to go to school. 'I always get a

sore throat before an important performance', translation: the muscles in my throat are all clenched up because I'm frightened I may not sing well. 'I've never felt so good', translation: the person I'm falling in love with makes me feel relaxed and carefree inside and out. In other words, involuntary muscle is strongly affected by the imagination. A voice which operates freely and efficiently is dependant upon the balance between the action of voluntary and involuntary muscle, between what you decide to do and what you feel.

When you were showing the little girl reading her book how to say 'moon', she could only observe the exaggerated movements of voluntary muscle involved. How could you demonstrate what was going on in mouth, throat, soft palate, tongue? How could you know?

Let your larynx do the talking

In my experience of dealing with words, use of language improves and develops as a result of strengthening the role which involuntary muscles play in articulation. Simply, this means that you stop talking so much with your face and start talking more with your larynx (where the vowels are formed), throat muscles, tongue muscles and soft palate. Your face is now free to take up its natural role, that is expressing what you are feeling. Zygomaticus and buccinator are muscles not of articulation but of facial expression. This chapter is mainly concerned with re-balancing the use of voluntary and involuntary muscles in your throat, mouth and face when you articulate words.

🖭 EXERCISE ❿ *Involuntary muscle at work!*

The photographs on page 89 were taken during the recording of this exercise. The sound engineer will vouch for this if necessary!

What to do

Pull your face about as I have done in the photographs on page 89. Then listen to what the song 'Drink to me only with thine eyes' sounds like when I sing it while pulling my face about like this. Then play the tape again and pull your face about vigorously while singing along with me.

I hope you discovered for yourself, during exercise 10, that the involuntary muscles of articulation are only awaiting an opportunity to take over whatever you want to say or sing with greater freedom, range of tone and variety of pitch than you might have thought possible. However, as most people have developed their use of language through visual copying I would advise that you spend some time now reading, or singing, aloud while pulling your face about with your fingers. It may come as quite a shock to discover that you can talk without involving your face at all. Language is important at a very deep emotional level. You learnt it when you were very young and from people who commanded a strong position in your life. Give yourself time to absorb this new information. The voice is always an emotional tool and requires gentle adjustment.

   Having released the face muscles from all but a minor role in dealing with words, the following information and exercises – about words themselves – are designed to stimulate your imagination, your throat, your soft palate and that most important of all the muscles of articulation – your tongue and its suspension.

Vowels and consonants

There are two basic sounds which make up both written and spoken language, *vowel* sounds and *consonant* sounds.

Common vowels are:

gAH
gO
frEE
lId
dAY
mOOn
tUck

There are others. Vowels can be sustained (said for a long time) and because of this they are the 'body' of language. Vowels are formed and sounded within the larynx itself with a little help from tongue and throat muscles. They provide the carrying power, the dynamics, your personality, change of pitch and emphasis. They express the *state* of you: nervousness, control, demand, authority, excitement. The sound of the voice is the sound of a succession of vowels.

What is a consonant? Consonants are all sounds which are not a vowel; they act as bridges from one vowel to another. Consonants are all short, hard sounds which should not be sustained and so should not be sung.

Count the number of consonants and the number of vowels in this paragraph and you will easily see that there are many more consonants. Consonants thus *appear* to be more important than vowels.

Syllables

Both consonants and vowels are organised into *syllables*. These are the building bricks of spoken language: when you say the word 'syllable' you say SI LA BULL. These three separate sounds which make up the word are its three syllables. Words can have only one, or many syllables. The first step in making sure that you move from vowel to vowel to vowel when you speak, is to consider how we build our reading from these 'syllable bricks'.

The syllable can be constructed in two ways:

● It can be a vowel as in: A – far
O – ver

● or it can be a vowel plus one or more consonants:
kIt–chEn
lIght–lY

Here is a sentence made up of single syllable words:
The sun has got his hat on.
Read it aloud. Say it again, this time *very* slowly. I am going to attempt to reproduce what you have slowly read.

THER – (which can be sustained because it ends with a vowel

SUNNNNNNNN – this syllable closes on to 'nn', closing your jaw with a snap

HAZZZZ	– this syllable closes on to 'zz' – another snap
GOT	– this one stops almost immediately
HIZZZZ	– another close down on to 'zz'
HAT	– immediate stop
ONNNN	– closes on to 'nnn'

Would it be reasonable to describe this sentence as a series of bites, because the final consonant closes the vowel off at the end of each syllable? This causes the jaw to snap shut.

Look at this:

THE SU – NHA – ZGO – THI – ZHA – TO – (N)

This is merely a rearrangement of the vowels and consonants to create a different syllable. (Note that when you read 'THI', in this instance you will pronounce T *and* H separately, *not* as in the word 'this'.)

Your jaw does not bite off the end of the syllable because there is no consonant at the end of it. Each syllable is now arranged consonant–vowel. This is achieved by moving the consonant which is normally at the end of the first syllable ending with a consonant on to the second syllable. Each syllable then begins with a consonant and ends with a vowel.

Look at the word 'photography'. Normally you would pronounce the word

PHOT – OG – RAPH – Y

This is the system which gives priority to consonants.

Now you can say

PHO – TO – GRA – PHY

which gives priority to the vowels.

Speaking is about sounding vowels. The voice moves from vowel to vowel to vowel.

THE SU – NHA – ZGO – THI – ZHA – TO – (N)

If you say this version very slowly you will discover that

you can sustain each vowel for as long as you wish because there is no consonant at the end of the syllable to cut short the sound.

Take up your pencil and notebook and write out some words for yourself. Write out each syllable separately. First write them out as you would *expect* to read them and check whether the syllables end with a vowel or a consonant. Rearrange them in open-ended syllables. Is there any improvement in tone quality of the voice when you change the way you read them?

Which is the easier version to sing?

THE SUN HAS GOT HIS HAT ON

THE SU — NHA — ZGO — THI — ZHA — TO — (N)

Which version encourages the jaw to be free? Check what is meant by 'free' in Chapter Three, 'Talking and Eating'.

Encouraging open-ended syllables

In Chapter Two, 'Out of Breath' there is an exercise called 'running on the spot' (see pages 46–7). This exercise is designed to change your attention from breathing in to breathing out. The arm-swinging movement in the next exercise can be used to practise linking open-ended syllables together into sentences.

EXERCISE ⑪ *Talking rubbish*

What to do

You are going to swing your arms rhythmically, as in 'running on the spot' (page 46) but instead of breathing out noisily on each swing, you are going to sound a different open-ended syllable. For example:

BA – MA – CHI – KU – LA – DAY – FRA – CRO – ROO – BYA, etc.,

one syllable for each swing. Listen to the exercise on tape first, then answer my 'rubbish' statement in 'rubbish' of your own. Keep the syllables open-ended!

Notes

By including inflexion as in asking questions or sounding puzzled you can make your 'rubbish' into sentences, breathing wherever you wish.

Further work

Repeat the exercise putting in as many variations as you can.

The next exercise on tape is to help you use open-ended syllables when you are reading 'real' words.

EXERCISE ⑫ *Reading the vowels*

Here is an extract from a well-known poem. You may not recognise it but don't try to do so. I would like you to read it as it comes. Here are the rules I have used in writing it:

1 It contains only open-ended syllables.
2 No letters appear which do not have to be pronounced, so some spelling has changed.
3 There is no punctuation.

I – WO – NDER – DLOW – NLY – A – ZA – CLOW –

DTHA – TFLOE – TSO – NHIE – AWE – VEH – LA

– NDHI – LWE – NOR – LA – TWO – NSIE – SAW –

A – CROW – DA – HOE – STO – VDA – NSI NGDA –

FO – DILS – A – LO – NGTHER – LEH –K BI – NEE

– THER – TREE – ZTE – NTHOW – ZA – NDA –
NCI – NGI – NTHER – BREEZE.

What to do

Read the poem as I have written it, out loud, continuously and slowly. Do not stop because you recognise the poem. Then play the exercise on tape, repeating each line after me. This will give you further ideas about how to approach open-ended syllable reading boldly.

Notes

I have deliberately chosen a poem which is usually spoken carelessly and much maligned in order to show you how you can experience quite a different 'feel' for language if you can only step beyond its visual representation – the words.

Further work

By practising this exercise and writing out your own choice of speeches or poems you will gradually begin to understand how words need to be allowed to change both in inflexion and tone relative to their grouping. Let punctuation fall naturally into place when you read the poem on your own for a second or third time, always allowing possibilities of change. Anything you would like to, or have to, memorise should be written out like this; you will discover that having re-organised the syllables and read a piece you will know it from memory. Write the syllables as you think they sound. This is how I have approached my own writing of the poem – it shows how the words sound to *me*, how *I* say them.

When you have read from the text to your own satisfaction, try singing the poem to a tune of your own invention.

The purpose of the last exercise is to make you very conscious of vowels. Consonants are merely the cosmetics of language: the buttons, the beads, the jewellery, meaningful but not structural.

From wobble board to balance board

As you become more adept with your wobble board, change over to the use of the balance board and try to use it to practise some of these exercises every day. Keep the wobble board for trying more difficult exercises from now on. The balance board frees the voice mechanism of so much daily habitual patterning and brings it to new life in a really wonderful way.

Here is another exercise for introducing a greater variety of pitch into your speech. It throws the voice action backwards and forwards between speech and singing, which gives it the most wonderful stretch in every way. This is especially true if you have a plant on your head, or stand on your wobble or balance board.

▭ EXERCISE ⓭ *'The vet who surprised a cow'*

This piece is taken from Stephen Pile's *Book of Heroic Failures*.

What to do

Read through the story, but *sing* all the words printed in capital letters. Sing them as low in pitch as you can, as far below your normal speaking voice as you can manage. You can try this first on your own and then follow me on the tape, or listen to me first for encouragement – whichever you prefer. Sing '£45,000' as well, when you come to it.

The Vet Who Surprised a COW

In the course of his duties in AUGUST 1977 a Dutch VETERINARY surgeon was required to treat an ailing COW. To investigate its internal GASES he inserted a tube into the END of the ANIMAL not capable of facial expression AND struck a match. The jet of flame SET FIRE first to some BALES of HAY and then to the whole FARM, causing damage estimated at £45,000. The VET was later FINED £140 for starting a FIRE in a manner surprising to the magistrates. The COW escaped with SHOCK.

Notes

Do not shorten yourself in any way in order to sing low in pitch. I believe the plant on your head and a mirror before you to be essential when you first attempt this exercise; this is to discipline your head to stay where it is. Perhaps you'd like to use the wobble board as well, just to be on the safe side. Obey the rules of all the talking/singing exercises: move from talk to sing without a break. You could sing two or three different pitches on the words in capital letters but always lower than speech pitch. If you have difficulty in dropping the pitch of your singing make a vigorous hitch-hiking gesture over your shoulder with your thumb as you sing. This exercises omohyoid and springs your vocal trampoline into action. Allow the sung sound not only to drop in pitch but, in your imagination, to drop back behind you as well, as though it were emerging from between your shoulder blades. This should help. Your speaking voice may well drop in pitch during this exercise. Allow it to do so.

Further work

Finally, read the story through normally.

Revision: exercising talking and singing muscles

You should be aware by now of two or three different ways in which to exercise muscles which are required in talking or singing. Here is a revision of some of them:

1   Lying in prone and reciting or singing.
2   Hitting the floor at the beginning of a phrase or sentence.
3   Shouting OI! at the beginning of a phrase or sentence. Don't try to make a polite OI! – remember someone is making off with your bike! Do not breathe between OI! and the first word.
4   Singing all the verbs (see also page 69).
5   Rewriting poems or prose in open-ended syllables or even reading with open-ended syllable construction in mind.

EXERCISE • *Revision*

Read the page of a book aloud, thinking carefully of open-ended syllables. Hold one cheek out and up as this will prevent the 'bite' of the jaw at the end of the syllable. Remember your voice is all vowel, the consonants are merely decorative.

Stumbling

Having exercised the voice thoroughly on the units of speech, it is now necessary to join them together, not in rubbish but in some intelligible way. When the desire to be clear and to communicate an idea exists, the mechanism often tries, fails, sounds at the wrong moment or does not sound at all. We may call this lack of confidence, stammering, stuttering. There seem to be two factors common to all these stumbling problems.

1 They do not happen in singing.
2 They increase with stress.

In singing, the larynx moves about more than in speaking: it also springs about much more strongly. (If it did not do this before you read Chapter One I hope it is beginning to do so now.) The tongue moves with the larynx, both being attached to the hyoid bone. In singing the tongue moves backwards and down, less of it being in the mouth, more of it having to articulate in the throat. In stress the larynx is pulled higher in the throat, creating a sensation of 'tight throat'. The tongue moves into the mouth so that there is less of it in the throat. In work I have done, both with stammering and with the voice in stress, the position of the tongue is crucial to the condition of the voice. It appears that the more you can strengthen and rebalance the tongue muscles, thus shifting articulation away from the front of the mouth where sucking occurred, the less the voice stammers. (See Chapter 12, Sandy, on page 192.) Whenever I work on a tongue its owner is always surprised. The back of the mouth is for most people a totally unknown area. The diagram on page 102 will help you get to know it.

This diagram shows the relative positions of tongue, soft palate, hyoid bone, larynx and spinal column. When articulation occurs at the level of the larynx the whole of the shaded area becomes throat for speaking and singing. The voice then stimulates sinus areas and nasal cavities, maintaining clear spaces in them. The tube connecting inner ear mechanism and throat is exercised by stretching of the upper section of the

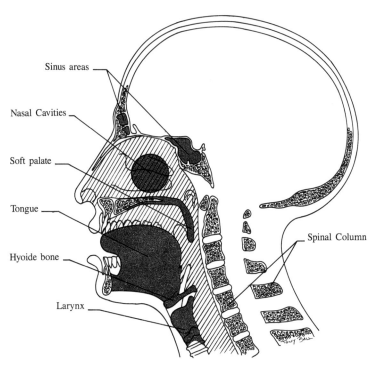

Your articulation equipment

throat. You then begin to listen to your voice from inside yourself as well as outside.

Take a few minutes to have a good look at your tongue. Poke it out and all round to find its full movement potential. Now lick around the back of your teeth, your soft palate and your tonsils. How much of the back of your mouth and throat can you examine with your tongue without being sick? Discover the different shapes occurring in the mouth and throat relative to this extensive tongue movement. Feel how your jaw and soft palate move relative to the tongue.

Look in the mirror and notice what shapes your tongue can make in order to perform these tasks. Watch your face and the changes to cheeks and upper lip caused by tongue movement. Discover as much as you can about your own tongue *before* reading on.

The tongue

We begin life sucking and this is one of our main activities for a long time. The sucking pattern is so strong that we keep returning to it all our life, in stress, for comfort, in moments of concentration, etc. Because sucking is such an important activity for the newborn infant, the tongue, larynx and hyoid bone, which you remember are all joined together, lie high enough in the throat for the whole of the tongue to be situated in the mouth. All the muscles of the tongue can thus be involved in the strong forward thrust which gives the tongue priority over the larynx for the first couple of years.

The tongue action is assisted by the pulling in of the cheeks and the pulling down of the soft palate. The suck is completed at the front of the mouth by a strong circular muscle around the lips. This muscle is responsible for what is generally referred to as the baby's 'rosebud' mouth. This position of the tongue in the mouth also allows the baby to suck and breathe at the same time, the uvula of the soft palate being close enough to the epiglottis of this high larynx for the two

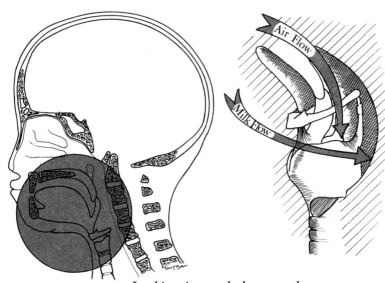

Looking into a babys mouth

to lock together and prevent the sucked milk from entering the larynx.

Sucking gives way to chewing when teeth appear. However, during the weaning period the tongue still remains in its position entirely within the mouth space and it is not until the age of approximately six years that the larynx, hyoid bone and tongue move to a lower position in the throat where, apart from modification during puberty, they will remain for the rest of life. (See: *The Human Vocal Tract* by Dr Edmund Crelin, published Vantage Press, 1987.)

How old were you when you learned to talk? Although I do not expect you to have an accurate personal memory of the process it is not difficult to calculate. Most children are fairly articulate at nursery school, at about four, more so at primary school at five. Many read very well by the time they go to school at five. I believe I can safely draw the conclusion that the action of speech is learned before the age of six. Speech is therefore learned with the tongue working entirely in the mouth in its primary sucking position. The infant voice is very high and breathy, not very loud except in temper, crying, screaming. The larynx pulls down during the shouting, crying or screaming into the adult position then returns when the bout is over. Between approximately six and eight years old the larynx, hyoid bone and tongue move down the child's throat, the tongue taking up its dual position of part in the mouth and part as front wall of the throat. After this change of position, articulation of consonants can also change. They can now be made further back in the mouth and throat, using a combination of tongue, throat muscles and soft palate. Speech and singing can then occur further down at the level of the vocal cords, which is where the vowels are produced in the larynx.

It is interesting that speech problems seem to begin around six years and intensify over a period of about two years after that. But if you learn to speak with your tongue, the main articulator of consonants, in one place and then find yourself having to adapt because it shifts position, perhaps it is not surprising that this age group suffers particularly. The modification between talking with the tongue entirely in the mouth and talking using the back or throat part of the tongue seems to happen most naturally and easily amongst children who sing before they can fully articulate and then sing all the way through learning to talk. The kind of singing which seems to produce the clearest and most freely articulate speech in a child of eight or nine and thereafter throughout life seems to be singing which is regular: every day – and fun.

I believe strongly that singing improves speech in every respect, provided that natural connections are maintained between talking and singing. The action of the tongue appears to be crucial to this natural connection.

Here are three pictures to explain how, as children, we begin articulating with the tongue in the mouth and how our articulation needs to modify to accommodate the adult tongue position.

There is a great deal of information to digest; some of it will come as quite a shock. Many people are working very hard to exercise the forward and pointing muscles of the tongue in order to improve pronunciation, articulation, communication. I am asking you to consider that

1 Vowels are made in the larynx with *some* assistance from the back of the tongue and throat muscles around the larynx.
2 Most consonants are articulated in the *same* area around and above the larynx by tongue, throat muscles and soft palate.
3 Of course the lips and teeth do play a part in articulation but it need only be a very small part.

Examine the three pictures very carefully and visualise your own use of the tongue. Whether it is constantly crashing into your teeth as you talk, if so, which teeth? The front ones or the back ones?

Much of the information in the three pictures will only become relevant when you have worked at the exercises on pages 111–13 so, once again, do not try too

STAGE I

Speech is developed with the tongue entirely in the mouth.

Primary function of the tongue is to suck.

Speech is mainly directed forward against the lips and teeth.

Singing encourages the adult position of the larynx and assists in easy movement to **STAGE II.**

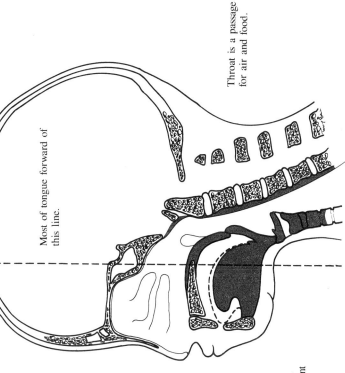

Most of tongue forward of this line.

Throat is a passage for air and food.

STAGE II

Approx. 6 years old.

Dotted positions of tongue, soft palate, throat muscles show interaction which an now produce consonants.

Tongue now lies mostly behind this line.

When sucking is released the back can become a soundboard for the voice.

Tongue and larynx drop back and down.
Speech modifies to new tongue position.

STAGE III

Development sometime after 6 years old (if allowed)

Co-ordination of tongue, soft palate and throat muscles develops to produce most articulared speech **behind** the dotted line.

In adults speech and singing are thus directed backwards onto the natural soundboard — the back.

Face and lip muscles mainly concerned with facial expression.

Vowels are formed in the larynx itself with the assistarce of tongue and throat muscles.

hard and do not expect to understand everything at once. If at first you merely question whether a tongue could *possibly* work more efficiently further back in the mouth, that will do to start with. Then begin the exercises and come back to the information with some ideas of your own beginning to formulate.

Before you move on to the exercises consider the following information once more.

Vowels are the basic structure of language and these are all formed and sounded inside the larynx. Place your hands around the base of your neck and imagine the bulk of your voice, both singing and speaking, being articulated in that area. The first vertebra of your spine is situated under the lip of your skull. Find this by poking your fingers around the top of your neck at the back whilst nodding gently. The vocal cords operate roughly level with the sixth vertebra. Find the sixth vertebra by putting your head down, chin on chest. The seventh vertebra will then become very prominent. Return your head to upright and find the next vertebra up. That is roughly the level of your vowels. Consonants are formed mainly between the larynx and the back of the mouth by that part of the tongue which lies in the throat, the throat muscles and the soft palate. Very little speech is formed in the mouth. The face muscles are for facial expression, not articulation.

Now go back to Exercise 10, singing 'Drink To Me Only'. Listen to the tape again. Imagine that you can say or sing all those words with the main focus lying at the level of your sixth vertebra. This would entirely free your face muscles to be pushed around, or to express what you are feeling, which is their prime function.

Tongue exercises

These are both tongue exercises and methods of allowing the vowel to occur as far into the larynx as possible while the articulation of the consonants occurs mostly behind the back teeth (or where the back teeth once were!).

The first exercise is not on tape. It uses the word AND.

EXERCISE • *On 'and'*

According to what I said earlier, 'and' is not a good syllable: it is not open-ended, that is, it ends with a consonant. If we put several 'and's together, however, it is quite simple to create open-ended syllables:

A — NDA — NDA — NDA — NDA — NDA — NDA — NDA — NDA —
(ND)

1 A   is the vowel and should feel to be continuous.
2 D   can happen right on the back of the tongue.
      Take your tongue back and up to begin. This will raise and widen the soft palate and widen the face below the eyes. (See page 115 third tongue position.)
3 N   should be considered an almost imperceptible bridge between them.

I have put the final consonants in brackets. Sing some tunes, ask some questions, using only 'and . . . and . . . and . . .' for the words.

Watch yourself in the mirror during the saying and

singing of this exercise. Your jaw should do nothing. If it continues to leap up and down whatever you do, take hold of a good handful of one cheek, lift it out from your teeth and up towards your ear. Now try. That should free your jaw from the last traces of the working of masseter (see page 71 in Chapter Three 'Talking and Eating'). When your jaw does *not* move about as you sing or say this exercise your tongue will be articulating in two places, at the back of your mouth and in your throat.

😐 EXERCISE ⑭ *'nayah'*

First of all try singing the two syllables of 'NAYAH'. Notice that you are singing NAY – AH and not NAYEE – AH. What is the difference? The difference is a *diphthong*. What is a diphthong?

What to do

Go to the mirror and say NAY – AH very slowly, watching all movement. Do your teeth close at the end of NAY and open again for AH?

Now listen to me singing 'nayah' on the tape. I am singing it while brushing my teeth! Have your own toothbrush ready, and then play the tape again singing with me and brushing your teeth at the same time. Brush the back teeth particularly.

Notes

Can you feel how differently your tongue operates when you are brushing your teeth? It changes position from Nay to Ah because the jaw is occupied. Moving the jaw excessively during speech causes some vowels to change before you have finished saying them. Thus:

> Play becomes Play-ee
> Blow becomes Blow-oo
> Tiger becomes Taheeger

and the more chewing in the jaw the more you will emphasise the secondary vowel. The secondary vowel caused by the movement of the jaw is called a diphthong.

When the back of your tongue becomes really strong and flexible, unwanted diphthongs will not intrude into your speech.

🗩 EXERCISE ⓯ *'gah'*

What to do

Push your face up either side of your nose – I appreciate how sore this is becoming but it is all in a good cause – spreading your upper lip and exposing the upper front teeth. Say 'GAH'. This 'gah' will be articulated well into your throat with the jaw remaining free. Now play the 'gah' exercise on tape and sing it after me like this until you know what to do with your tongue.

Further work

When you have performed this exercise with your face pushed up, try doing it while brushing your teeth: remember to concentrate on brushing the back, top and bottom teeth.

Now it is time for you to locate some specific tongue muscles so that you know which parts of your tongue are performing various different movements. Arrange a mirror and a light so that you can see *into* your mouth. Check each tongue position with the photograph. This will give you a greater tongue control and clearer articulation will follow.

The tongue's muscles

First position

The tongue is attached to the jaw in the floor of the mouth. Stick your tongue out as far as you can and then move it around wherever it will go. Repeat the same movements inside the mouth and back around the soft palate. This is usually very easy for everyone as 'making a tip' is a primary tongue position. If you weren't able to do this you probably would not have survived because you would not have been able to suck.

Second position

The connection with the hyoid bone. Pull your tongue back and down at the same time. The tongue forms a dish shape in the back of the mouth. It is what you do when the doctor places a spatula on your tongue and tells you to say 'Ah'. Can you feel how restricting this is? It stiffens the whole larynx, pressing it down in the throat. See what happens to your face, neck and jawline. This is your vomiting action for the tongue.

Third position

The two sides of your tongue are attached by a muscle to your skull – see diagram on page 116. This is a very important muscle in the process of speech because it moves the tongue back in the mouth and also up into a

First position (left)
Nothing difficult here

Second position (bottom left)
Tongue pulled back and down.
You can see the back wall of the
throat

Third position (bottom right)
Tongue pulled back and up.
Tongue has lost its tip

position where it can work with the soft palate and
throat muscles in articulation. It also connects the
action of the tongue to the action of the larynx as both
are connected to the styloid process of the skull. You
began to use this muscle only when you had finished
sucking and the tongue moved into the throat; if you
have retained a speech action which uses the tongue
excessively against the front teeth, this muscle may not
be working at all. It is called *styloglossus*. It attaches the
tongue to the floor of the skull. Strengthening this
muscle automatically strengthens and widens the back
of your neck.

Styloglossus suspends the tongue back and up. This
is a position which seems difficult for most people to
move the tongue into. I find the easiest way to

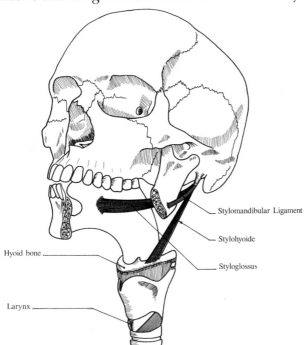

Hyoid bone

Larynx

Stylomandibular Ligament

Stylohyoide

Styloglossus

Muscle connecting tongue to skull

approach this tongue position is to locate your back teeth – upper set! – and touch both sides at the same time with your tongue. You do this when you are cleaning your teeth, so sing Exercise 14 'nayah' again with the tape while keeping a toothbrush at work on your back upper set. Observe your tongue in a mirror as you sing this exercise. Are you surprised that you can have a toothbrush in your mouth and also sing?

Your whole speech efficiency and fluency will improve if you strengthen all the muscles of the tongue. The weakest of these in my experience is always styloglossus, which pulls the tongue up and back, suspending it from the skull. It is weak because it does not become effective until the Stage III development shown on page 109. By then we have already learned to talk. Increasing the work of styloglossus rebalances the tongue muscles. You will then be able to give priority in your speech to the vowels. Strength of voice is developed through vowel priority.

⌨ EXERCISE ⓰ *'Come, sleep'*

This is your first opportunity to devise a work programme for yourself using a poem. The poem is on page 206.

What to do

First of all, listen to the poem on the tape. Keep in mind that the vowels should have priority and the consonants act as decoration.

You are now going to design a short 20-minute work programme to help you perform this poem to your own satisfaction. Write down the exercises you decide to use, to increase your confidence, enjoyment and control, in your notebook. Do your programme once a day for a week.

Notes

Here are some guidelines to help you devise your programme.

1 Always begin by balancing yourself in some way before you talk and sing. This could be use of the balance board, or lying on the floor for five minutes, or observing your breathing quietly.

2 Always include an exercise to link up breathing and voice in an efficient way. This could be the talking rubbish exercises or some singing exercises.

3 Do some moving between talking and singing using any poem or prose of your choice. For instance, sing the verbs, sing a line – talk a line, or sing

some words on low notes as in Exercise 13, 'The vet and the cow' on page 98.

4 Always do some exercise to free the jaw and tongue, for instance, pushing the face around, lifting one cheek alternate sides, pushing the face up, using a toothbrush.

5 Always move through all these procedures *before* you begin to decide how you would *like* to say the poem. In this 20 minutes of work all kinds of possibilities may emerge just by the freedom you give your voice in the workout.

After a week of working on your programme, write down your observations and note any changes in your voice. Keep this note in your notebook after the outline of your programme.

During the week still work on your tape. That work is quite independent of your work plan for 'Come, sleep'.

When you have completed this chapter and the week's work on 'Come, sleep' you might find it useful to go back to Chapter Three, 'Talking and Eating', page 62, to link up all your new information on the tongue with information on the action of the jaw.

6

Adrian

I held a series of workshops in London for non-singers and discovered what a tremendous loss it is for many people when they believe that they cannot sing. The variety of occupations represented at these classes was staggering. Very few had been concerned with music making of any kind, but all longed to sing. In one class there was an infants' teacher (retired), a TV cameraman, a museum curator, a public schoolboy, a couple of secretaries and a car salesman.

The car salesman, Adrian, worked for a very upmarket motor manufacturer based in London, and commanded a good salary with a standard of living to match. He did not know why he wanted to sing – he just knew he did.

At some point I always introduce voices to the 'Singing The Verb' exercise which you tried out on page 69. We hide behind so much social patterning and this is an ideal exercise to allow the real voice to emerge. It cuts through the games we play with our voices by throwing our habitual voice action into confusion. I put Maurice Sendak's book *Where the Wild Things Are* on the stand, balanced a plant on Adrian's head and he began on the first sentence: '. . . Max

woooooooore . . .' His singing of the verb could have
been better. Breaks between singing and talking. Start
again. He struggled for a bit with the idea that he
could move from talking to singing *without* stopping –
and then suddenly he had got it. The next phrase he
performed was another voice, another man. It had the
strongest Birmingham accent you could imagine; just
like that, no preparation, another voice entirely. He
stopped and took the plant off his head. 'I've always
been afraid that would happen sometime,' he said. 'It's
as though that other voice is fighting to get out all the
time and I have to hold it in.' Why should he feel like
this about his voice or the way he speaks?

I invited him to alternate, one phrase Birmingham,
one phrase indeterminate Home Counties, and
discover how easily he could make the choice from one
to the other. He was surprised that he had the choice
and *could* choose. When he was choosing to alternate
these two voices he discovered that he could sing in his
Birmingham voice, easily and in tune. This voice was
deeper and his face muscles were much more relaxed.
He was funny in this accent, as though this voice
contained his sense of humour. The other voice, the
one he began the course with, was rather more
pompous, and he admitted that it was what he referred
to as his 'professional voice'. He used it for work,
interviews, sales, telephone. However, these two voices
gradually influenced each other as he swapped them
about, so that the professional voice dropped in pitch,
tension released from the face, and he began to be able
to sing in that voice too. As the day wore on it was more
and more difficult to distinguish one voice from the
other and Adrian began to sound natural, with his
voice now containing the naturally acquired inflexions

which all our voices possess if we let them.

How had this man acquired two voices? His parents were both doctors, practising from their home in Birmingham. The neighbourhood where he grew up was a tough one but this was not a problem in his early years. He mixed easily with local children. However, at seven his parents sent him to a prep school in another area. Adrian described graphically his arrival on the first day at school, how he heard all the children at school talking 'properly' and realised that there was a fair chance of taking some bullying because of his own speech. 'The first boy that spoke to me, I spoke back to him in the same way. I kept it up all day. It was easy. I didn't think about it – I just did it. When I went home at the end of the day I spoke like myself so that I fitted in there too. In one day I learned to have two voices and use them for the two people I had to be, one at school and one on the streets at home. I never thought about it.'

He kept that up as a system all through junior school, 'Birmingham' at home, 'proper' at school, until he finally went away to senior school as a boarder when he merely adopted his 'proper' voice as his own. He had subsequently moved to London where his lifestyle and his job encouraged what he now knew to be 'received pronunciation'. However, he had originally acquired this pronunciation in quite a tense situation, and, as Birmingham was the first language in which his voice had learned to talk, his second voice was not so relaxed. The tensions in this manner of speaking made his vocal trampoline too rigid to spring about easily and prevented him from singing.

Adrian saw that both these languages were part of him and he was no longer subject to those childhood cruelties which originally caused him to hide his accent. He was, in fact, very pleased to find it again and allowed his 'professional' speech to expand to include expressions and inflections from Birmingham.

Having two or even several languages is fairly common. Many people have a telephone voice until they know it is not an official call. This is not the same as having a voice flexible enough to tune in to the conversations of other people so that you make them feel comfortable. The quality of Adrian's voice was vastly improved when he allowed some 'Birmingham' in. It was more colourful and he smiled more when talking. The change in his voice seemed more aligned with his lively personality – and of course he could sing, which gave him enormous pleasure and satisfaction.

Adrian was a salesman. His professional role can be compared with that of an actor or a teacher. All are selling their wares by word of mouth. All need to sell, be it a character, a subject or a motor car.

Teachers, salesmen, actors and many other professionals are practising the art of salesmanship. The simple mechanics of salesmanship are that you:

1   identify the audience, customer, class, in terms of need, ability, receptiveness;
2   apply your stagecraft, sales technique, teaching, in such a way that those listening to you feel confident that the voice reflects your sincerity.

The flexibility of your voice is imperative to point 2. A free voice will produce the speed, inflexion and language to deal with each special case. A good actor will begin the first moments of a play differently on Monday, Tuesday and Wednesday because when the curtain is raised the silence or lack of it is informative. The voice behaves differently on each night although the words are the same. If this interaction between mind and voice is not available to the actor, the play will only succeed when the audience fits the interpretation which has been rehearsed. Flexibility of voice allows the actor to begin the play wherever the audience can be captured and then, throughout the evening, draws them along the path the play wishes them to tread.

Similarly, the salesman needs to be able to talk TO rather than AT his customers. Speed, dynamics, intonation, are all variables in the art of selling. In a situation in which the price of goods, the salesman's suit and the product itself all remain the same from customer to customer, the voice is often the only flexibility possible in the sale. It is then important that the salesman has a voice which is not one exclusively trained in the delivery of prepackaged sales material. Salesmanship is a natural endowment of a voice which moves easily between speaking and singing.

It seems to me that there is a message here for the salesman, the actor, the teacher and anyone else who is concerned with the art of communication.

There are aspects of your voice which you can use for different situations, and the decision to use them is controlled and contrived, as with Adrian and his two voices.

The danger of vocal games is that over-indulgence can be such a habit that the voice loses its spontaneity and you may lose touch with your true voice.

I wonder if Adrian sold more cars when he put his two voices together?

In Tune —

Out of Tune

One of the greatest blocks to singing is the fear of singing out of tune. Anyone who sings out of tune is assumed to be tone deaf and anyone who is tone deaf, unmusical. Just as people are divided into singers and non-singers they are also divided into musical and unmusical. If you believe that you are tone deaf you do not want to be heard attempting to sing. Better to say that you do not sing or that you do not like singing, inferring that you *choose* not to sing.

What do the terms 'out of tune', 'tone deaf' and 'unmusical' really mean? What is actually happening to the voices of people who sing out of tune? Is it possible to cure this condition and thereby become musical, having been unmusical?

I have actually been both musical and unmusical, sung in and out of tune at different periods of my life. I therefore know that it is possible for one voice to behave efficiently or inefficiently, depending upon your understanding of how it operates.

This is how I believe it happened. When I was small I learned how to learn. With an overwhelming curiosity I collected information from every source available, never selecting but gathering all. I listened, looked, questioned, talked to others and myself.

Somewhere in me this information was sifted, stored and acted upon or forgotten without my having to worry about any of it. I never thought of mistakes. If they happened, as they must have done in this haphazard gathering, I was not aware of it. I then went to school and over the next ten years my learning habits were changed. I was channelled into those things I could do and out of those things I could not. Comments on school reports encouraged me to believe that:

A I should be ashamed of mistakes
B If I tried very hard I would not make mistakes

By the age of seventeen I was convinced that success was entirely based on:

'Practice makes perfect.'
'If at first you don't succeed, try, try again.'

I then decided to train to be a singer.

I absorbed all instruction, learned masses of repertoire, took every conceivable opportunity for self-advancement and, by this method and my guiding rules, I reached 30 singing out of tune with a voice that could have sliced through metal and an attitude to life that made mincemeat out of friends and colleagues. The complete failure I experienced was, in a way, the sum total of all the little failures, mistakes and misunderstandings which I had avoided in my 25 years of formal education. That is not to say that school and music college were not good for me or that what I learned there was useless, but that *being correct* was too important too soon and the greater proportion of my attention and energy was occupied in maintaining my path to success and reward.

Eventually, of course, came the occasion to end all others. I sang the soprano solo for Mozart's 'Requiem' in Coventry to a packed hall. The work begins with the chorus repeating 'Requiem Aeternum' until the soprano soloist enters with a single, beautiful phrase, 'Te decet hymnus, Deus in Sion', which I heard myself singing – flat! Mercifully this is followed by six pages of chorus, but there was no mercy for me sitting there and knowing that I had the rest of the work to perform with a voice out of tune, uncontrollable, and therefore, by definition, unmusical. Needless to say that was my last professional engagement and my first acknowledgement that something was seriously wrong. Memorable though!

Had I been given a voice test at that time I would have been judged tone deaf, out of tune, unmusical. How can both states, musical and unmusical, exist in one person in one lifetime? Half a lifetime! My confidence was severely shaken.

There were other distressing signs of this misuse of the voice. I was also a schoolteacher at the time and I frequently became 'voiceless' or exhausted.

I do not sing out of tune now and I do not lose my voice. In my years of training I had been working on my voice and the music which it performed. But what I had missed was the fact that my voice belonged to a whole living system. The mind, body, emotions, fears, affect the voice as, in turn, the voice will affect them. When I accepted this fact and introduced it into my work my voice became a 'strong' voice because I was then working with a much broader understanding of what constitutes 'strength'.

All of us experience times when we feel we are dropping apart, unco-ordinated, out of balance, out of tune. If we do not understand the natural mechanisms of the body but allow personal problems to interfere with balance, posture or breathing, then not only is it difficult to deal with those problem areas satisfactorily but the voice, which is the most delicately balanced of our natural mechanisms, will show signs of wear and tear. There are two common signs of that wear and tear, singing out of tune and constantly losing your voice. These problems indicated that I had lost control of *myself*.

When I looked beyond the problems of singing out of tune I noticed that I had the following additional difficulties:

1 When I tried to sing I experienced breathlessness, sweating and palpitation of the heart.
2 I suffered from sore throats, laryngitis, tonsilitis, colds, sinus trouble, general stuffed-upness, in a chronic and irritating cycle.
3 My speaking voice acquired a rasping quality. Even close friends backed off a little!
4 My balance had gone. It was only when this lack of co-ordination began to improve as I worked on my voice that I realised how often during this period I tripped over kerbs and pavements. I could step off a bus poised and smiling and the next minute I was flat on the floor after turning my ankle or falling over my own feet. I called it clumsiness but later recognised that my *whole balance* was poor.
5 I could not be wrong. When I was 'ticked off' or politely taken aside for advice I would laugh, shrug, apologise and quip: 'Must take some time off. I'm getting tired.' Or 'Had a long slow drive here. My dress is tight. My feet hurt. It'll be back to normal tomorrow.' When I regularly lost my voice at the

end of term I blamed the unruliness of 4B or the impossible timetable or the problem of running both a home and a career. I would have a rest, a panic, practise like mad, get someone in to clean my house and convince myself all would be well. Because I could not be wrong I closed my eyes to the real problems and looked only at those problems I could sort out myself without help. If that did not at first improve the situation I stuck at it until I had struggled through.

I believe that many people experience the speech problem – losing the voice – but do not realise that they have also lost the in-tuneness of the voice because they do not sing and so do not hear it. When one function of the voice is out of tune then so is the other and an out of tune voice is one not operating efficiently in any activity. So if you are one of the people who say 'I couldn't sing in tune' you must begin work on that now.

I have worked now for 20 years with out of tune voices. In each case I have asked pupils when it was that they discovered the voice was out of tune. All too frequently it has been in early school life at the age of seven, eight or nine.

When a child gives up singing at this early age there is little chance for him to take it up again at any time during school life, or indeed during adult life. Singing is generally lost for ever, often in the space of five dreadful minutes. The mind equates the activity of singing with an unpleasant experience, like burning your hand on a hot plate or catching hold of barbed wire. That wonderful connection between voice and imagination is limited and a rather dull speech can result. What limits vocal expression is the rigidity of the whole trampoline system. The panic associated with out of tuneness can be replaced with the real pleasure and satisfaction of knowing not only that the voice is in tune but what keeps it there. It is *understanding* which creates confidence and tuneful singing.

Let us return to the questions at the beginning of the chapter. Do the terms 'tone deaf', 'unmusical', 'out of tune' all refer to the same condition?

Yes. In all cases it is the use of the vocal mechanism which is at fault.

It is nothing to do with your ear. There is nothing wrong with your hearing mechanism. When I play a note on the piano it is that note that you will hear. Now if I ask you to *sing* that note you may well sing something different. You will then call yourself tone deaf. But the answer lies not in the ear but in the vocal spring system and the larynx which must co-operate in a precise and balanced way before you can repeat the note you heard. It is when this co-operation is absent that you may well sing a note other than the one I played.

Here are some other reasons for inefficiency of the voice mechanisms:

- Ignorance of what is required – the singer receiving incorrect instruction in how the voice works.
- Fear.
- Emotional difficulty.
- 'Startle pattern' (see page 56) occurring at the moment of singing, thus stiffening the voice mechanism.

Now consider the logic of each supposed condition of out of tuneness.

1 Tone deaf or deaf to pitch

Can you recognise individual voices on the telephone, a case when you have no visual aid for guidance? If so, aren't your ear and brain making fine discriminations of tone, pitch, rhythm?

How do you speak? If you are deaf to pitch wouldn't you speak on a monotone? What gives your voice variety in speech if it is not one of tonal and pitch selection?

Can you recognise the difference between a Northerner, someone from Birmingham, an Indian, all reading the same instructions? How do you manage this if you are tone deaf?

When you say 'Darling!' does it sound the same as when you say 'I'm afraid this road is private!'? If you *are* tone deaf presumably it does!

2 Unmusical

Why do we apply 'musical' only to those who *do* music and never to those who listen and like? A child who is judged unmusical at seven, eight or nine is unlikely to be given a chance to learn to play an expensive musical instrument. Singing is so often the test for natural musical ability. I have met few people who went on to play instruments having learned that they sang out of tune. Music has, then, to be a passive pleasure for those who do not sing.

This book contains the information and exercises to reforge the links between ear and voice. There is no need for you to sing out of tune any more. The path to being in tune and therefore musical is fun and the world of singing which it opens up to you will bring you such joy and pleasure. However, it would be an enormous step towards developing widespread confidence and self-esteem if out of tune singing was not established in the first place. Prevention is quite simple. Children can all be encouraged to sing at home and at school, at least once a day in each place. Parents could sing round the house. Mothers need to be encouraged to sing to their children from infancy. When children are tested in school it should never be for vocal efficiency. That will come with use and growth and development. Voice tests should be used for entering choir schools – where musicianship is the criterion – not school choirs which should have a less specialised approach. Children who can sing will emerge naturally from a system where the class is the choir, the choir is the class.

Singing to movement can be encouraged. Operas improvised by the class from stories or events being studied will improve vocal use by enhancing overall co-ordination. Improvisation also encourages everyone to find a natural pitch level. It is much better and more fun for children to stand in a ring so that they can walk or skip around while they are singing than it is for them to stand in an orderly group facing forward and focusing on paper in their hands.

In your notebook, jot down your early singing or non-singing experiences. What do you remember? Who encouraged or discouraged you? What did you enjoy or hate about singing? Do you sing out of tune at the moment?

Johnny

Johnny was seven, at a primary school which encouraged music. There was a musical specialist on the staff. Johnny sang out of tune and his voice was much deeper and louder than any other voice in his class. When there was singing Johnny gave out the books and often tidied or re-organised the music cupboard. He might play percussion instruments as he seemed to have a good sense of rhythm. However he was generally disruptive in the music class, showing off, pulling hair, flicking paper. Of course Johnny might well have been just a naughty little boy, perhaps spoiled or perhaps lacking attention. Both extremes can be responsible for this kind of nuisance.

I met Johnny because he came to play with my two children. When four or five local children were somewhere in my house consuming biscuits after school Johnny would appear in the music room and fiddle with the piano. In an effort to find him something to do while I worked I taught him two tunes on the piano and as we sorted out the notes of these I learned of his problems with singing. This little boy obviously felt left out and inadequate in these singing lessons, even at his age.

I noticed that when Johnny sang, the attitude of his head changed with high or low pitch and the whole of his body became tense. He clutched his hands together and his bottom tightened, hollowing his back. His jaw was never free. The very thought of singing induced this state in him. We worked by singing and throwing bean bags around, singing and hitting the floor, in fact doing lots of the things which appear in this book, except that his balance board was a skateboard.

Johnny has now grown up. The photographs on pages 134–6 are of another boy called Thomas. He also sings out of tune and contorts himself just as Johnny did when he sang. It is eight years since I worked with Johnny. It is disturbing to realise that there is still no improvement in the attitude to out of tune singing and that Thomas displays the same startle pattern on which I worked in Johnny eight years ago. Look carefully at the photographs. All the work in this book is based on combining the balance and poise of the boys on the skateboards with the activity of the voice. Thomas will not sing in tune until he is able to discover that concentration is not the same as 'trying' and the body and the mind should be co-operative and give each other feedback all the time. He will then experience the ease and sense of fun which is so obvious in the final photograph. When this happens, his singing will be in tune and his adult speaking voice will develop tone quality and flexibility, because the voice will *spring*.

Here are some particular points of observation.

● **Photographs 1 to 6**
Permanently clasped hands. The jaw is not free in any of these shots – see Chapter Three, 'Talking and Eating'.

The mouth shows a distinct sucking attitude throughout, indicating that the tongue may be pulling into the mouth to talk and sing. Each note has a different head position largely related to pitch. In Photograph 2 notice the hollow back and rounded shoulders. Compare this bottom with the

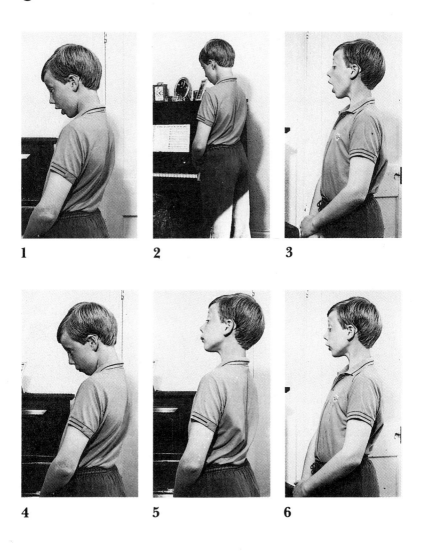

1   2   3

4   5   6

bottom in Photograph 8. In Photograph 3 the chest
is lifted and tightened, which would indicate that he
'takes a breath'. The pelvis and belly are also pushed
forward.

7

8

9

10

11

12

- **Photographs 7 to 12**
  Not one example of clasped hands. Well they would
  fall off, wouldn't they? Photographs 7 and 9 are
  Henry, Thomas's brother. Note the different view
  they have of concentration. Thomas tries hard and
  'over-trying' may have led to his out of tune singing.
  These are all about balance and stretch.

- **Photograph 13**
  A wide open mouth but a tight jaw. He is using biting muscles to sing. Compare the length of shoulder to waist with Photograph 8 taken five minutes after.

- **Photograph 14** is listening – a collapsed activity for Thomas.

- **Photograph 15** is singing – a tense activity for Thomas.

13   14   15

Musical

Singing in a choir is very much like playing football for your town or belonging to the local field club. Not only is it an opportunity to do something you enjoy doing anyway, but you gain friendship, mutual support, a sense of responsibility, self-respect and a great deal of laughter and fun. And, what's more, it's good for you. You can arrive at your practice feeling really tired and dispirited and after singing for only about ten minutes you will feel quite different, lively and energised. During that ten minutes breathing improves and the whole body experiences a good stretch. Singing is a very concentrated activity. The voice is our most complex system. It is quite impossible to sing well and simultaneously worry about last month's figures. There are few activities which relieve work stress so effectively.

The voice does not age like the skin and the bones. If the springs of the vocal trampoline are well exercised and co-ordinated the voice will retain all the vitality and expression which is within you. When competitive sport is well behind you singing will still give you immense pleasure, as well as keeping you fit.

Out of tune voices are voices which have cut themselves off. You do not listen to yourself because you believe the sound to be awful and you do not listen to the required pitch because you do not believe you will achieve it. That is the cut-off between brain and voice.

The act of having to put these two awful moments together, as Thomas is doing in his singing photographs, produces an extreme physical response, an intense startle pattern. That is the cut-off between body and voice.

Communication is severed, you sing out of tune. If it is a speaking moment you may stammer. All the following exercises work on three directions:

1 Listen to yourself.
2 Listen to others.
3 Avoid startle pattern.

As these three activities are interfered with at an unconscious level, I don't want you to *try* too hard to do them. I am sure that by now you have worked out that the simple and apparently frivolous exercises in this book are all designed to make improvements, not only at a conscious level but at an unconscious level too.

These exercises must be done with someone else; sometimes you may need a group. A group can be three people. I leave you to organise that. Do not imagine that you will not benefit from them if you believe your voice to be trouble-free. Working on your voice with others will expose any problems you may still have in communicating.

EXERCISE • *Back to back*

This is for two people. One assumes the role of teacher and one pupil. The roles are interchangeable.

Sit back to back.

Teacher now says: OI!

Pupil repeats it on the same pitch as quickly as possible. Do not take a breath to start, you do not need to.

When these OI!s have gone back and forth for a

Soften the backs together

Look ahead

while and the backs have softened and moulded together, the teacher begins to *sing* the OI!s and the pupil responds again as quickly as possible.

Check that the backs remain together and that the heads remain balanced easily, the eyes looking out in front.

Aim to give the OI! and its 'echo' response in sets of five or six pairs, no time in between.

This will become a 'catch-you-out' game, but as the game develops ensure that you maintain the easy sitting and the contact through the backs.

Variation:

1 Play the game with the teacher as observer and the pupil on a wobble board – rocking it like a boat – with plant on head. Point out any stiffening – (well

they'll probably fall off anyway) or any glazing of the eyes.

2 Play the same game hitting the floor and pointing at each other to sing. Stand at either end of the room to do this.

3 Try giving a two or three syllable word with a different pitch to each syllable. The response must be a *different* word with the *same* number of syllables and the same pitch, eg:

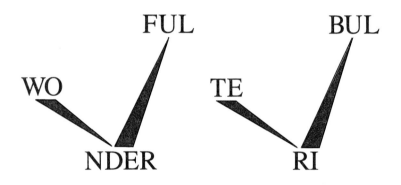

(Open ended syllables, of course.)

EXERCISE • *Singing your name*

This is a group activity (a group could be three!).

Stand in a circle. Everyone says his or her full name aloud. Always make it into a game. For instance, one can volunteer to start and then throw a beanbag to the next name to be given until all have given their names. Explain what a syllable is. Call it a *building brick* for talking and singing. How many building bricks in each person's two names?

Examples: An-Ge-La Caine = 4
Su-San Har-Ding = 4

The beanbag is thrown again and this time each member sings his or her name with one different sound for each syllable. There must be a slow demonstration for this and it may take several rounds before everyone sorts out the syllables, but a great deal is being co-ordinated in this exercise:

- Staying where you are
- Deciding to begin
- Facing a group
- Communicating with someone else
- Selecting pitch
- Deciding to change pitch

These are some of the neglected but important decisions which need to be made when using the voice in any context.

There are many variations to this game once it is mastered by the group.

Allow members to change their names to one they would prefer. Make rules. The name must go continuously up in pitch, down in pitch, up, down, up, down. Let the group enter into a game of catching each other out. Always move to the next name by throwing a beanbag.

Be patient: do not care about musicality and above all make it fun.

After two or three sessions something will begin to emerge. The group will begin to relate. The voices will copy and clash and experiment with one another, just as a group of people will do. Then they can be guided.

They can be encouraged to start on the finishing note of the previous name, to sing that note longer so that it *can* be passed on, meanwhile pointing at the person who is to take it up. Encouraged to make their own games, they are singing without the fear of singing the wrong pitch – and that is the beginning of all singing. If you then move on to a group discussion you will be astounded at the breadth and originality of ideas which will emerge, because all communication tracks will already have been opened before the discussion begins.

EXERCISE • *Singing or talking to the wall*

Everybody leans on the wall, as in the photograph. The hands and elbows hang from the fingers – just enough finger pressure to keep them there. The

You could hold a conversation with someone similarly positioned across the room. You will be surprised at how lovely your voice sounds when you speak or sing in this position

forehead leans lightly on the wall. Maintain a body line all the way from ankles to top of head but do not tighten your buttocks to achieve this.

The group leader sings a tune which is *recognisably* the first line of a well-known song. The group is told what the song is and that this is the first line, for instance the first line of 'Baa, Baa, Black Sheep'. The tune is sung again, everyone still against the wall where they have been listening, and this time they are told that the last note will not be there – they must supply it and in this position.

EXERCISE • *Lying on the floor in semi-supine*

Gravity is a very strong influence on the head/neck relationship. The head is balanced on the top of the spine in such a way that it requires only delicate activity by small muscles to keep it there. However, if we stiffen and shorten the back of the neck, gravity becomes too powerful a force for those small muscles to counter. Lying down removes that strong force and allows the small balancing muscles to recover.

F M Alexander was an Australian actor who developed the Alexander Technique from observing the problems he had with his voice. He continuously lost his voice while reciting and discovered that the habit of pulling back his head and thereby shortening the back of his neck created the conditions throughout the whole of his body which caused the breakdown in his voice.

One of the activities recommended by many teachers of the Alexander Technique is lying for 20 minutes a day in semi-supine.

You need three or four thin paperback books as the head needs to be supported. Then you lie on your back with the books supporting the lip on the back of your skull which overhangs the neck vertebrae. This is easily found by your fingers if you nod your head a little. Choose the thickness of support by what is comfortable if you turn your head left and right. The neck curve is now suspended and can release a little in the 20 minutes you lie there. For maximum easing of arm and leg joints, place the hands on the tummy, elbows bent, and raise the knees into a bent position, the feet flat on the floor shoulder-width apart – shoes off, of course. (Look at the photo.) You could attempt to sing in this position. It is a position of maximum release and minimum tension, and the larynx is in a very good position for talking and singing.

Practice speeches, poems, presentations, plan meetings in this position.

Semi-supine is also a good position for bulking up the discs which separate the vertebrae of the spine and give many people so much trouble. To lie down in the middle of the day is to give a boost of energy to the spine which counteracts back pain and tiredness at the end of the day.

⌨ EXERCISE ⓱ *Lying in prone*

What to do

First, listen to me on the tape. I *am* lying down and singing! You can sing anything you like, or use 'Twinkle, twinkle little star' and 'The sun has got his hat on' which you have sung before.

Now lie face down on your stomach with your forehead on the floor. If this is very painful on your nose turn your head for a while to the right – cheek on the floor – and then to the left. The arms can be down at your sides or out in front, elbows bent. Allow your legs to do whatever they want, feet falling in or out as is comfortable. You need to be there for five minutes at least, longer if you can, so that:

the shoulders can release;
the pelvis and hip joint can release;

3 your weight can be allowed to fall into the floor.

When you have lain there for your five minutes sing a nursery rhyme, preferably with forehead down. Begin your song by talking the first line and then, without taking in any more air, go straight into singing the second line, thus:

SAY: 'Twinkle, twinkle, little star' (no breath)
SING: 'How I wonder what you are'

Do not judge yourself. Try it a couple of times with different simple tunes and then give it up until you next lie down to do this exercise.

The Voice & the Motor Car

Seventy percent of the adult population regularly drive motor cars. Some spend as little as 15 minutes on their journeys but there are many who spend about four hours a day behind the wheel merely getting to and from work, much of that time stationary, waiting for the car in front to move.

What do you do with this time? Many of us can only sit there with the adrenalin level creeping up as frustration sets in. Stressed motorists, realising the need to maintain a degree of attention sharp enough for the moment when the traffic moves on, devise various in-car diversions to prevent mind and body sliding into a dreary fog of boredom.

Our concentration span is generally quite short. There has to be a break before the level of attention is regained. Driving without attention, or even with reduced attention, is dangerous. Added to this problem of sustained concentration there are all the unexpected delays to deal with.

There is a very good argument for using your driving time to work on your voice. I designed the tape with this in mind. This is how it works.

The first side of the tape

You work first of all at home from book and tape, using the plant on your head, the two boards, and all the other paraphernalia while you learn to associate talking and singing with the tape while pushing your face around, hitting the floor and hauling your tongue around the back of your mouth. When you have absorbed the exercises for some time and associate them with these activities, you can use the tape in the car and, hopefully, as you sing each exercise you will, by association, activate the muscles you have used while working with the tape at home. As you repeat the appropriate exercise from the tape while sitting in the traffic, your pelvic floor will spring into life, your shoulders will widen and the ribs expand as they did at home when you hit the floor. You will also associate the singing with the explanation of what is happening which you discovered in the book. Thus, by alternating home work and car work, the whole system of memory and recall is exercised with the voice.

I consider the car to be an excellent place to work with the tape, both from the point of view of the voice and also to help the sharpening of driving attention.

As the voice becomes more mobile and flexible, the eyes and eye muscles are stimulated. Eyes need to move and see clearly and accurately both in main focus and peripheral vision at all times, but this is particularly important when driving. Voice work in the car encourages looking and *seeing*. Looking and *seeing* encourages free and lively singing.

The second side of the tape

One of the problems of driving for a long time is that of remaining in one position. However, when you are singing and remembering the connections between the flow of sound and the spring system of the vocal trampoline, all those parts of you concerned with producing that flow of sound are being energetically stimulated. Thus, by remaining in your driving seat, you can exercise muscles in the shoulders, the back, the diaphragm and ribs, the throat and back of neck, the face and tongue, the eyes, the abdomen, buttocks, pelvic floor.

The songs on the second side of the tape are for you to enjoy singing. Apart from the arms and legs which are continuing in a relaxed and free manner in the activity of driving, you are receiving a pretty good workout when you sing these songs. No slumping into a sleepy, dangerous stupor.

It is easy to develop the habit of frowning when concentrating. It has nothing to do with concentration except that many believe any kind of thinking is necessarily 'hard work'. Frowning, which is tension in the face and neck muscles, can cause headaches. You don't frown when you sing, at least not when you are working with this book! The face opens and widens. No clamped and angry jaws either.

The lights turn against you – *again!* – the main road is diverted, you have a puncture. After a bout of singing the jaw should be free throughout all these trials and tribulations. In spite of them you arrive ready to give of your best in work or relaxation, without the tensions which you might have gathered on the way.

The most important reason, however, is that you need to develop a high degree of attention. No-one can quarrel with that. You need also to revitalise that attention regularly when you drive for long periods and also at those times when you just sit.

Attention is a dynamic activity; that is, all your faculties are not only at their individual personal best, they are also interacting one with another. You are listening, looking, thinking, physically alert and springy, arms and legs freely and easily performing their various independent movements. When you have been driving for four hours the patterns have become set; you may still feel attentive but the dynamism has gone. The one activity which instantly awakens that dynamism and which re-centres the interaction between all those faculties is to have a really good, hearty, connected sing. Because you are responding to a tape the eyes are free to concentrate the vital attention and co-ordination developed by singing, on the road conditions and the resultant demand on the reflexes.

When I ask people whether they sing they often answer 'Only to myself'. I then ask 'Where do you find to do that?' The answer to that is usually 'In the bath!'

Why do people like singing in the bathroom? It is empty and lined with hard surfaces which enlarge and enhance the sound. Everyone feels like an opera singer. It is also a safe place. The door is locked or at least you can usually lock it. You feel warmly and safely cocooned. Is this not what you feel when you are alone and driving along in your car? Do your ever wonder at the driver who abuses you merely because you want to change lanes? Is he really so aggressive, or does that safe place produce a power which eludes him outside it?

> Motoring aggression is on the increase.
> Inattention is on the increase.
> Accidents are on the increase.
> Something needs to change.

Try working on your voice in the car. Do the exercises. Sing the songs. See what happens. You may begin to enjoy driving again. Singing may even slow you down. Before motorised transport people sang as they walked to market or drove in their carts. Armies always sang as they marched into battle to lighten their hearts and sharpen their wits. For many the journey to and from work has become a battle. Singing could transform it.

Private practice rooms available. Soundproof, heated, some with air conditioning. Cassette facilities

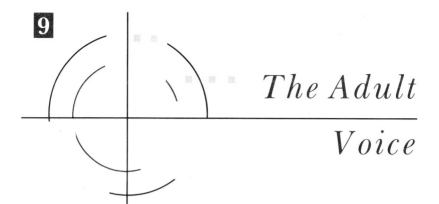

9

The Adult Voice

The voice changes gradually throughout our lives relative to personal experience. There are some changes which occur, however, that are common to all voices and happen at specific times. These need to be recognised and understood. It is quite unnerving to experience strange sensations when you talk or sing and to feel that this familiar part of your person has ceased to be reliable. If you know why it is happening you are less likely to panic. The first response to panic is to 'take a breath' and you have already learned that taking a breath impairs co-ordination.

A child's voice changes in puberty to an adult voice. This occurs both in boys and girls. The child's voice is usually higher in pitch than the adult voice and the quality of the child's voice does not vary. Thus a child will say 'I love ice cream' or 'My pet rabbit died yesterday' with exactly the same voice and it is this quality of innocence, of artlessness, which is so appealing when a child performs emotional material, such as singing Christmas carols or relating sad stories. The adult voice is deeper, in both men and women, and can change in quality to match different emotional states.

The growing voice

In Chapter One you discovered the position of the larynx in the throat. Place your hand around the front of your throat and locate the bony ridges of the rings of cartilage. Picture the tongue, soft palate, hyoid bone and larynx in yourself. Move them all about with a few drain noises. Try sucking very hard to feel what happens to your soft palate.

From the age of six to the age of approximately fourteen, the springs of the vocal trampoline are growing and strengthening. This co-ordinated system supports the demand made by a mature adult voice.

1 Shoulders grow and strengthen, the omohyoid muscles become flexible and strong.
2 Increased knowledge and use of language exercises tongue and soft palate.
3 Sporting activities exercise the lungs and breathing systems.
4 The pelvic floor becomes stronger and more active. The dual role of the pelvic floor as a spring for the vocal trampoline and the location for increased sexual awareness forges a strong link between voice and sexuality.

At about 14 the larynx enlarges; the human vocal trampoline has by now developed enough strength to support its greater weight. The development of the adult voice can now begin. Strange and unexpected noises often occur in boys' voices. Girls' voices become husky or loud and coarse. We say 'Your voice is breaking'.

The enlarged larynx now moves about more in

speech and singing. Make some drain noises with your hand around your throat, waggle your tongue, moving it in such a way that you can feel how much of it lies in your throat. Imagine what a long way the larynx has travelled if, at six years old, your tongue was entirely in your mouth and your soft palate could reach your epiglottis. These changes of position and size in the human vocal trampoline are usually completed by about 14 to 16 years old and the voice has dropped in pitch. At this point the voice is often thought to have completed its changes. However, there are still adjustments to be made and we need to understand them if we are not to cause interference in singing and speech in the adult.

Firstly, this new, deeper, heavier voice must exercise itself on all the repertoire of language which has been stored in the memory by the *child's* voice. Throughout the next few years the ear and imagination must grow accustomed to the new sounds and to the new and greater possibilities of tone colour, dynamic (for example, the volume) and pitch. The tendency is for the teenager to use this bigger, rather awkward and harsh voice as little as possible due to embarrassment at the strangeness of it, especially at school. Great encouragement is necessary if the adult voice is to work itself into place. Unfortunately much of the syllabus presented in school, in both literature and language, not to mention foreign languages, is too sophisticated, too subtle for the awkward action of this newly acquired voice. Seeds of hate for good literature and for attempts at foreign languages can be sown in this period of fourteen to seventeen when the developing adult voice is strange and new and fails to cope with complexities of rhythm and pitch. There is little time in which to 'voice' everything so that the ear and imagination can become accustomed to using this new and exciting instrument. Ideally, the voice needs improvised drama sessions, debate of all kinds, lots of singing and the patience and encouragement from all to build confidence. This early period, 14 to 17, is the most important for establishing familiarity between person, voice and material; a bit like having a new bike with twice as many gears as your old one. You need to get the feel of it for a while before you go anywhere special.

The emotional voice

The adult voice can also express emotion in the tone quality of the voice. Because we have this emotional quality at our disposal we are able to use words in a much more subtle way, conveying more than the mere words themselves. During puberty a special blood supply develops as a part of increased sexual awareness. This blood supply is highly oxygenated and is controlled by hormones, responding to sexual or emotional excitement. It is the special blood supply which erects the penis in the male and the vulva in the female. It swells tactile tissue, for example, the lips, lining of throat. Tactile tissue is that which has a very thin, transparent covering, as in the inside of the mouth. The vocal cords also receive this blood supply, which produces an adult, emotional quality of voice.

These are the child to adult changes which occur in the vocal cords:

The child's voice is operated solely by air pressure

passing between two stretched cords or membranes. Take a rubber band and stretch it so that the two halves of it lie side by side. This gives you a good idea of a child's vocal cords.

The air pressure changes to change the pitch of the voice – the vocal cords remain constant. Blow up a balloon and pull the neck in the same way as you pull the rubber band.

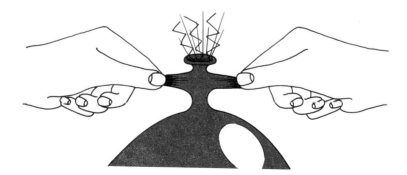

By experimenting with pressure on the balloon you can make the pitch of the 'squeak' rise and fall. A child's voice works like this balloon.

Then the voice breaks, the larynx enlarges and the special blood supply is connected to the vocal cords. The vocal cords themselves can now change. They become more or less erected by more or less oxygenated blood, according to the emotional stimulus. So the adult voice does not operate by increasing or decreasing air pressure in order to sing higher, lower, louder, softer, etc. The adult voice sounds as the result of a very delicate co-ordination between the erection of the vocal cords and variable patterns of breathing. The muscles of back, ribs, pelvic floor, soft palate and the central breathing muscle, the diaphragm, all achieve a delicate balance which allows air to pass over the erected cords at the correct pressure for any subtlety you wish to communicate. This is why taking a breath and consciously controlling your breathing is such a disaster in any voice use. Simply exercise the voice well and maintain a regular balanced work programme and the rest will fall into place.

There is, however, one way in which everyone can co-operate to encourage the efficient balance system between breathing and the erection of the vocal cords. The adult voice requires very little air to sing or to speak, much less than the bicycle pump action of the child's voice. Many of the exercises in this book are designed to reduce the amount of air you believe you have to 'push' against the voice in order to activate it. Now that you have had the adult voice action explained to you, you could consider very carefully:

1 NOT taking a breath before you talk or sing;
2 getting in touch with your breathing by listening to it for a few minutes each day, not with any desire to change it but merely to discover that reflex,

described in Chapter Two page 52 'Out Of Breath', which breathes in for you when the moment to do so is right.

The readjusting voice

The change which occurs between child and adult, which we call 'breaking', can now be considered as a period of readjustment. That readjustment will occur naturally, if:

1 talking and singing are encouraged throughout the maturing period, whether the voice is at its best or not;
2 everything is allowed to adjust – pitch, weight of voice, breathing; no preconceived ideas of how you would *like* your voice to be;
3 the maturing period is allowed to last for as long as it is required. How long is that? How long is a piece of string?

The most successful attitude to have is to allow the child's voice to disappear with all its limitations, and then tell oneself 'Here we go. This adult voice I am meeting at fourteen will develop all the way through my life. I shall exercise it and play with it, read aloud and sing, stretch my spine and increase rhythm and spring in the supporting trampoline. Where will it take me, I wonder?'

A general guide is that the child's voice has usually disappeared by 14 to 15 and the adult voice is settling down by 23 to 24. This may seem a long time to you, particularly if your voice broke one day in choir practice and you considered it done. But your voice is very important to you. It is well worth allowing it to become stable in the following ways.

- Physically   through the spring system of the vocal trampoline.
- Intellectually   through the use of language, music, conversation, and so on, with the greatest variety of material possible.
- Emotionally   via the special oxygenated blood supply.

A connected adult voice creates confidence in speaker and audience. It is a pleasure to use and a delight to listen to.

Has your voice matured?

How do you recognise in yourself a voice which has not completed its adult maturing period?

1 Out of breath problems with speaking and singing. The breathing has not adjusted to the adult vocal cord. Consequently the whole voice is over-pressurised; you may be hyperventilating. There are many exercises in this book which encourage this adjustment.

2 Difficulty with singing and moving, walking and talking, working and talking, losing your voice when tired. The vocal trampoline is not operating strongly enough to support the larynx. Perhaps you always sit with your legs crossed, or hunch your shoulders, or stiffen yourself.

3 Lack of 'play' in the vocal machinery. Difficulty with accents, foreign languages, imitating giants, witches, dragons, ghosts, etc. General unimaginative use of the voice. You probably do not sing. These are qualities which develop from singing.

4 Difficulty with learning and repeating from memory. This can be a learning difficulty, but certainly a stable voice and good learning technique are *both* necessary, so if you feel stupid because you can't cope with a ten minute speech without a prompt, you may have a disconnected voice.

5 Are you a woman with a small, recorder-like soprano voice which has a very limited range? Many singing teachers refer to this voice as the 'Head Voice'. When you are singing in this so-called 'Head Voice' do you sometimes experience a shift in the machinery of your throat? As though a large lump has dropped about three inches? There is then a complete change of sound as though another voice has begun to operate. It is generally referred to as a 'break' in the voice. Many teachers attempt to match the two different sides of this 'break' by the singing of interminable scales and exercises, but there is no future in it. The 'shift' will always be a threat to your singing and this will destroy your confidence. The voice has never been allowed to adjust to the adult relationship between breath and erected vocal cord. The whole system is overpressurised and rigid. Singers with this problem have often been subjected to lots of breathing exercises or have sung complicated or heavily ornamented music while still very young.

6 Tenors with thin, passionless voices who are unable
to move when they sing have usually sung as trebles
in church or cathedral choirs. Again, the voice is
under too much pressure to allow the adjustment
between breath and vocal cord: the adult action is so
different from the treble voice with which they
began singing. If the eye gains supremacy over the
ear the vital adjustment between ear, imagination
and the new adult voice is not very successful. This
situation is brought about by too much sightreading
and not enough improvisation and fun. Voices need
to play. After all, voices are part of us, and *we* need
to play.

7 Infill. Builders' 'infill' is material used in
construction which has no particular aesthetic or
structural purpose. It is merely rubble. Vocal rubble
is *'sort of'*, *'Like – er'*, *'kind of'*, *'well – er – actually'*.
These phrases indicate a blind spot in the sentence
where the imagination/voice connection is
temporarily lost. If the connection between the
imagination and the voice is not very strong a
situation exists rather like a short on an electrical
circuit. Now and again you lose what you are saying.

Example without infill: 'I don't agree with that. If
Kate feels that David would be happier at another
school and she is prepared to make the necessary
arrangements, we should go along with it.'

Example with infill: 'Er – just a minute. I don't
think I – sort of – quite agree with that. Er – I'm
sure if Kate – er – kind of – feels that David would
be – actually – happier at – er – another school and
she is – er – sort of prepared to make the extra – er –
well – arrangements, we should – actually – go along
with it.'

How do you 'kind of feel'? What is the difference between 'going along with it' and '*actually* going along with it'? If you listen to conversation this, sadly, is very common.

Exercises to connect the voice

- Physically
- Intellectually
- Emotionally

The voice must be encouraged to continue its maturing process. We need to stretch the trampoline system and strengthen the connection between larynx and pelvic floor. We also need to make a strong connection between speaking and singing.

This means working hard on the first section of this book and also on the following exercises.

⌨ EXERCISE ⓲ *'Caro'*

What to do

First of all, listen to me singing this exercise on the tape. 'Caro' is Italian for 'dear one', 'darling', 'lovey' – any endearment which you use, so sing with affection. As you have heard on the tape, there are two versions of this exercise to help those whose voices will not at first extend very far. Now study the notes and the accompanying photographs. Practise the stretching movements and then . . . sing with me on the tape. Sing only what you feel able to do, then listen, and gradually add a little more.

Notes

It is the movement accompanying the exercise

which will release your larynx and gradually bring the singing into line.

First, take off your shoes. The photographs illustrate the movements you are going to make while singing.

I This is the starting position. Note that the feet are shoulder-width apart and that although the fingers are reaching upwards there is no raising of the shoulders.

2 Stretch one hand upwards as far as you can, pointing the fingers.

3 Release that hand and stretch the other hand. This creates a seesaw in the whole shoulder girdle. As the right hand stretches, allow the right knee to bend by bringing the heel off the ground and bending the foot. This creates a stronger stretch on the right side and also stretches the pelvic floor.

4 Replace right knee and repeat
with left knee and a stretch in
the left arm. Check this
exercise in the mirror to note
position of head throughout.
It should be balanced and still
with the eyes focused on
something interesting across
the room. Note the rhythm of
the movement in relation to
the rhythm of the exercise.
You are giving omohyoid and
the pelvic floor a strong
stretch and also co-ordinating
their movement.

(Can you still visualise
where these two springs are?
If not, look back at pages 31 and
32.)

This stretching exercise is also a very good movement
to use when reading aloud or saying a poem. It is
helping to programme your use of the whole of the
spring system when your voice operates. When
reading aloud, keep the rhythm of the exercise strictly
regular and observe your ability or difficulty in
reading something which has no regular rhythm. It is
important to good voice action that you can allow these
two apparently opposing activities to happen
simultaneously.

[⊞] EXERCISE ❶❾ *Children's story*

It is better to do this exercise in pairs as it is even more enjoyable – in fact it makes a good party game – and you need a little help with turning the pages of the book as well as someone to observe and someone to observe you.

What to do

Take off your shoes. Get your children's book and stand, your plant in a pot and your balance board. Now listen to the tape. I am reading from my chosen book, and singing the verbs as I come to them. You will do the same with a passage from your book. Listen to the tape again put a plant on your head and stretch right up. If you have just done exercise 18 you will feel a strong stretch right from the bottom of your ribs. That is good. Tell that stretch to stretch some more. Put the plant down and read a few pages of your book aloud. Go back to the beginning and now *sing* each verb as part of the sentence.

Only the verb is sung.

For this exercise to be beneficial as well as fun there are several points you should observe as follows.

Notes

Observe the following in each other after you have made the first attempt at 'singing the verb':

1 Can you change from speak to sing without having to stop the sound and restart it?
2 Can you change from sing to speak without having to stop the sound and restart it?
3 Can you manage one? Both? Neither?

Now have a second try at the exercise, keeping the following points in mind:

1 Slow down the changeover. Speak slowly and keep the sound of the last word going while you mentally decide to change to singing or speaking.
2 Keep the singing pitch the same as the talking pitch until the change has happened.

Then 'whirl' the pitch of the verb about and return to talking pitch: you will find it is now possible to return to talking without a break.

Finally, listen to the tape again. *Think* the instructions while you *listen* and *look* at the exercise.

Now try the exercise for a third time and aim for continuity. You may not achieve this first time. Do not try, try, try again. Have a couple of shots and then leave it for another time.

When you do come back to the exercise, try it with the plant on your head. You are going to look silly, so get used to the idea before you start! Make sure that the stand on which you have your book is high enough so that,

in spite of your new stretched-up height, you can still see it. When you have mastered some of the story you are using watch yourself do it in the mirror – plant on head, from memory, still singing all the verbs. Let yourself be really silly when the mood takes you!

Further work

The diagram below represents the relationship between the pitch of singing and that of speaking.

Speaking is the continuous line, singing is the dotted line.

Many people believe that singing is *above* speaking, but you talk in the lower *middle* of your voice range. Singing pitch is above *and below* talking pitch.

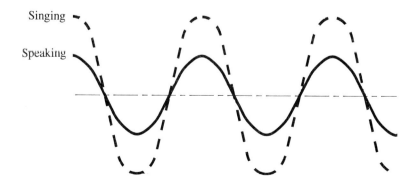

This information may make it easier for you to allow the singing of the verb to move both above and *below* the speaking voice.

When you have had a few attempts with a plant on your head, also stand on the wobble board (bare feet) with the plant on your head, read the story and sing the verb.

Remember that it is better to work with someone else. One of the side effects of this exercise is that you get to know the person you work with really well! While one attempts the exercise, the other can answer the following questions – when they have finished laughing at you.

I Are the sentences continuous, moving between speaking and singing *without a break*? Of course you may stop for punctuation as and when you normally would when reading.

2 Is the singing of the verb imaginative enough? Could more expansive singing be managed? (and still come back to talking without a break!)

3 Is only the verb being sung, or is there a tendency to go on singing *after* the verb?

4 Have you noticed anything changing in either speaking or singing?

Whenever you have finished playing with this exercise re-read the section in which you sang the verb, just speaking. Is there any difference?

What kind of voice have I?

I am often asked 'What kind of voice have I got?' This question is really 'Am I a soprano, baritone, tenor, etc.?' or even 'What kind of a tenor am I?'

As I said at the beginning of this chapter, your voice is subject to changes just as you are yourself. If you subject your voice to a narrow vocal repertoire your voice will become limited and inflexible. A diet of early music is not better than a diet of pop music, either will reduce your range of colour and flexibility. Similarly we tend to use a repertoire of spoken language which serves to communicate within our own work, friends and interests. The worst harm we can do to our voices is not to stretch them and stimulate them. I am, therefore, reluctant to classify voices, because you immediately have expectations and expectations are in themselves limiting. It is too easy to say 'I don't sing those songs because I am a soprano' or 'My voice would not be right for that character, it needs more weight'. I would hope to encourage you all through this book that your voice is always capable of more than you have tried so far. We have not even begun to use voices.

I would, however, like to offer some simple guidelines, because many people working with this book will be in charge of voices: school teachers, choir trainers and conductors. When the adult voice first emerges it is baritone in the male and mezzo soprano in the female. Both these terms mean middle of the road. They are the most common voices and *all* voices begin with this central pitch range. Thus, if you took 500 sixteen-year-olds and put them into one vast unison 'sing' they could *all* sing the Russian Folk Song which is chosen for its middle range.

As personalities develop in young adults, some voices move outside this middle pitch range. The voice shifts up or down. But there may be a temporary or false shift, just as the seventeen-year-old brings home a boyfriend totally unsuited to her and pursues the relationship through hell and high water until one day she says 'I've finished with him. I can't bear him!' This is why it is important to allow the voice its full seven years to sort itself out so that it can experiment and retract if necessary.

Below is a note of the names given to the range (highest to lowest) of female and male voices. It is important to realise that there are no fixed limits for each 'class' of voice: there is a central band of pitch which all voices share.

	female	male
The highest voices are:	soprano	tenor
The middle range of voices are:	mezzo soprano	baritone
The lowest voices are:	contralto	bass

The main difference between these voices is not one of pitch but of colour.

Before leaving the adult voice there are one or two loose ends to tie together.

Using your balance board

There is a strong connection between the way in which you use your legs and the way in which you breathe. Some of the main muscles of your upper leg attach into your spine at the place where your diaphragm inserts, thus affecting its function.

When you consciously control the breathing, it is necessary for you to stiffen your pelvic floor and some of your leg muscles. The legs become fixed.

The balancing board sorts this out beautifully. When you have mastered standing on it – try singing on it, sing anything, songs, singing the verb, work on the tape – while balancing. It is a different item of vocal

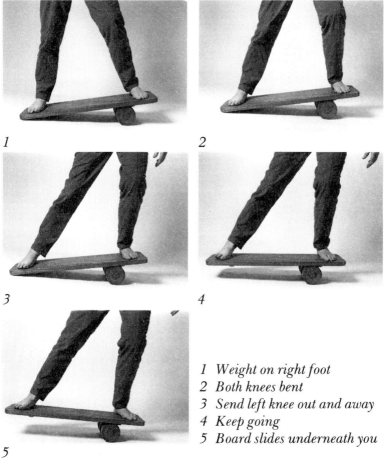

1 Weight on right foot
2 Both knees bent
3 Send left knee out and away
4 Keep going
5 Board slides underneath you

equipment from the wobble board, although I have advised you to begin on that as there is less chance of falling. You learnt to move the wobble board with knees, hips and ankles bent; keep this flexibility as you try out the balance board. Balancing can produce an excess of fear, so take it slowly and gently. Be easy on your own efforts. If you tense unnecessarily or consciously control your breathing you will immediately lose your balance and fall off the board.

Place the wobble board in front of your mirror and watch how you balance. Have a look at the photographs on page 11 where all the contributors to this book are standing either on a wobble board or on a balance board with a plant on their heads. You achieve this balance by sending your head away from your feet. Give yourself that instruction and discover whether your balance improves. *Now* you can *sing* on the board. Try the Russian Folk Song.

Using your back

When your back is really working well, your breathing is being exercised by bending and squatting and the extra expansion of the lungs by the widening of that back. Then, using the same system – you talk or sing; *not* by learning to do something else or consciously controlling the breath.

Singing and reading

Collect a repertoire of rhythmic, fun songs. Cole Porter, Gershwin, Lloyd Webber, Rodgers and Hart, Flanders and Swan, Tom Lehrer; songs which have good tunes and words but which you do not associate with musical detail or subtle pitching or phrasing. You are more likely to be able to review your musical 'programming' while singing this kind of music. Write the words down and then sing the song from your copy of the words. It is better not to follow notes which you sing. You are then less likely to stiffen because you do not *see* the pitch going up. Sing as much as possible without a copy. Be wrong if necessary and correct yourself by *recalling the sound* rather than by *looking at the music*. When at a loss, improvise. Read aloud to yourself or to someone else. Listen to the sound of your own voice, not so that you can like or dislike, but so that you recognise it and observe changes in it.

In a world where almost all information can be manipulated or turned on its head, the voice remains a means for every person to communicate on an understandable and reliable level. A voice has the potential for leadership in a way that a mechanical device never will. Examination Boards are recognising this and changing many of their tests to oral assessment. This is not confined to school and further education: for instance, if you want to enter the Police force part of your interview may involve giving a talk on say, cats, or transport, or maybe yourself. At any level of promotion you may be giving a presentation and that will be a deciding factor in your future. If society is going to expect everyone to be articulate in public it is only fair that everyone should be given some training in it. Imagine what could happen if you extended the group of three which works together on the voice to a large group, say a class at school or a department at work!

The second side of the tape, with the songs, may have eluded you so far. Have another shot at it when you are next stuck in traffic, picturing the three ways in which the voice is considered adult:

physically   intellectually   emotionally

10

Suzanne

uzanne was rejected for the choir
when tested at nine and didn't care,
because anyway she hated singing
and music and all that stuff. She did
not get much encouragement, but
neither did she ask for any. She was
attractive, dominant, outspoken, and
at school popular and well-liked, though not always by
the staff.

Although she had never sung in a group at school,
by the age of 12 to 13 she was collecting pop records
and spent all the money she ever had on the
paraphernalia associated with the 'pop scene'. This
horrified her parents, because although they were not
particularly encouraging, they loved her and wanted
the best for her. They looked at the pop music interest
and saw:

- It commanded more attention than school and
  home added together.
- It was tuneless, noisy and transient.
- The people producing it seemed to follow doubtful
  and immature lifestyles.
- It was accompanied by antisocial, antifamily
  behaviour.
- The lyrics were sexually stimulating, apparently

encouraging drug-taking and anarchy; criminal behaviour appeared to be acceptable.

Suzanne's voice was using pop music to achieve its changes. The very tunelessness of it allowed her child's voice to lose its pitch repertoire and wander aimlessly for a while through music which will never last long enough to programme the larynx in any way. Suzanne, by her interest in pop music, was fulfilling many of the requirements of the maturing voice.

The voice needs to be unstable and to experiment with uncontrolled, harsh, loud noises as it 'breaks'. She was allowing her voice to behave the way it felt. At school Suzanne found only music in which her voice felt uncomfortable. The emphasis seemed to be on tuneful beauty and that did not match the strong, rebellious statements her voice wanted to make now that it was connected to her strong teenage emotions.

So the first part of the maturing of the voice was achieved. She let her child's voice go and used her awkward, rather coarse adult voice. Her parents threw up their hands and tried to ride out Suzanne's adolescence with a sense of humour, looking forward to the day when she 'settled down' or 'woke up' or 'saw the light', or whatever phrases parents use in this situation.

The next stage was the stabilising of this emerging voice. It needed adult material to stretch itself on. A good drama teacher could possibly recognise this, but what about the girl herself? She had a reputation in school for missing school activities to attend local pop gigs. She was rebellious, often rude. She would probably let you down – better not chance it. She was too awkward, too unstable.

Suzanne developed very large breasts at about 17. This became an acute embarrassment – it happened so suddenly. Before that she was skinny, loudmouthed, sporty. She wore short skirts and possessed a commanding, arrogant voice. Suzanne advertised her potential sexuality but, like the pop music, it was awkward and easily forgotten. Suddenly she had large, embarrassing breasts. She hid them by caving in her chest so that they were not so noticeable. She carried her school books in front with folded arms; the shoulders hunched and the disguise was complete.

Because Suzanne did not understand how her voice was connected to the rest of her by the human vocal trampoline she allowed the spring system to collapse. The head moved forward with the shoulders, omohyoid muscle doing no work at all. The blood supply connected to the vocal cords but what can the voice achieve without its support system? Suzanne collapsed from top of head to feet. She was probably a good inch shorter than she should have been by the time she was 19.

Suzanne completed her education and her training, but she found herself in adult life feeling that she had more to offer in some direction if only she could discover what it was. I met her casually at a party. 'I gather you're a voice teacher. I'd love to be able to sing, but I haven't any voice and anyway I can't remember words or songs. I'd be a *real* challenge to you because I don't even sing in tune.'

There was a great deal of work to be done to put some spring back into her voice. Much of it had to do with rolling around on the floor and using the balancing board. It was only when she discovered that she could only balance if she sent her head up into the space above her that her shoulders began to sort themselves out. She sang the verbs with a plant on her head and discovered she actually had a voice which she quite liked. She only had to get to know it and spend some time with it and it began to work for her. This was the area of potential she had previously missed.

There is another habit which needs consideration and which develops during puberty.

This is crossing the legs. Girls begin to sit cross-legged as sexual awareness increases. The pelvic floor cannot then function as part of the voice action. While I realise that it is a very common habit, there are certain times when you could uncross your legs, place both feet on the floor and your bottom securely and evenly on the chair:

1 When answering the telephone.
2 When being interviewed.
3 When answering questions.
4 Any time you need to sound confident, cool and assured. (Usually that is exactly when women cross their legs!)

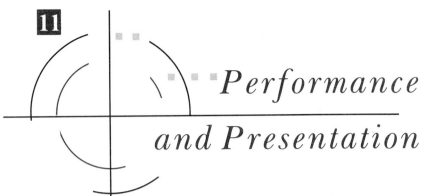

11

Performance
and Presentation

The work in this book is cumulative. This chapter comes at the end because success in performance is dependent upon several very simple guidelines which free your energy and imagination to flow into the material you wish to communicate. These simple guidelines are usually sabotaged, however, by tightening the jaw, exaggerating facial movement, taking a breath. The choice not to do these things must be strengthened *before* putting yourself in a position where you need to deal with memory and recall.

So, keep returning to those relevant chapters and the simple exercises, keep reading about Michael who controlled his breathing, about Adrian who was not himself, about me who was seeking perfection.

Then the simple exercises in this chapter will help you to communicate with more than one person at a time. That is the aim with which to begin any work on performance.

Look at the photographs. Have you heard this one? But all this arm waving and dancing from foot to foot can be distracting. Would *you* take his advice?

Do you wish you could do before an audience what you did so successfully in rehearsal?

'You should have heard it this morning.'

The work in this chapter demonstrates how the demand of walking on to a platform and communicating with a group of people affects the way that you think and behave. And that includes taking lessons, going to auditions, and even answering the telephone. It then shows what you can do to control these responses.

We must first ask some simple questions.

1 What is it that you believe you have to do to achieve good performance or presentation?
2 What are the demands which you have to deal with?
3 Is there a focus for your attention and concentration which controls these demands?

We need to deal with these separately.

Question 1 What is it that you believe you have to do to achieve good performance or presentation?
I include here acting a role, making a speech, demonstrating or lecturing.

Usual answer: Prepare the material carefully and accurately, with plenty of rehearsal. Learn, if possible, from memory. Rehearse with any co-performer (for instance a pianist) so that you both know what you want to convey. Plan questions, the position of visual aids, lighting, and decide on the amount and planning of the space required.

This answer is good but it only rehearses and prepares the material. What about the rehearsal and preparation of you? Putting on a suitable dress or suit is not enough. What you do with your trembling knees, stiff arms and flashing smile is going to affect your voice and hence your delivery, so carefully rehearsed.

Question 2 What are the demands which you have to deal with?

Usual answer: Remember the words, or come in at the correct place in the music. Remember to stand well forward. Remember to turn off the lights. Think of my first line. Make sure my cue cards are in the right order. Remember not to talk too quickly, and so on.

Again, this is all to do with attention to the material. There is no consideration of *how* you are standing, only *where* you are standing. *Looking* at the audience does not necessarily mean *seeing* the audience.

Question 3 Is there a focus for your concentration and attention which controls all these demands?

If I asked you what you were concentrating on more than anything else as you faced your audience, what would be *your* usual answer?

> Trying not to panic
> Breathing deeply
> Trying to be alert
> Projection of myself or of words
> Courage
> Memory
> Self-control
> Experience

If you concentrate on any aspect of these 'hooks' or you stand offstage murmuring words or allowing a song to go through your head, you will walk out before a group of people and hope to communicate with them while relying exclusively on the memory of what you did yesterday. Now how can that possibly work? Yesterday's information is not relevant to this live situation today.

There is a great deal of information on how to prepare and rehearse your material. My intention here is to show you how to communicate it in an immediate and flexible way, not by concentrating on the material but by concentrating on yourself and observing your audience. I believe that this can be achieved by giving yourself four directions at the moment you face your audience:

STOP   OBSERVE   LISTEN   BE ALERT

Stop

This must occur when you come face to face with your audience. It is very rare for a performer to do this, and I realise that when you consider walking into a space, turning to face a number of people and standing still, the prospect seems alarming. However, be patient, you have something to do to help the situation. As you walk towards the place where you are to speak, or sing, there will be much to stop. For instance:

STOP   remembering the words
STOP   remembering your first line
STOP   trying to stand in the right place
STOP   preparing anything
STOP   straightening your tie
STOP   moving from foot to foot
STOP   clearing your throat.

When you have stopped all that and anything else you are thinking about you will be ready to begin.

Divide your weight equally between both feet; be aware of your feet spreading on the ground, toes lengthening out in front, weight on heel, big toe joint, little toe joint. Take time to do this. Give it your attention. Stand still, and silently.

Practise this before a full-length mirror. Walk into view and stand. Watch yourself cope with standing **still** but not **stiff**.

Look

When the eyes do not focus, the voice does not focus. Many people refuse to look at their audience, preferring to gaze vacantly ahead or watch the clock or exit sign at the back of the hall. However, you need to look very carefully at your audience. As you look carefully at them ask yourself questions about them. They are, after all, your guests.

● How many are there and where are they sitting?

● Are they looking forward to this or are they looking bored?

● Are they cold, hot, comfortable, uncomfortable?

● How far away are they?

None of these questions have to be answered, they merely have to be asked as you stand for a moment of STOP before your audience. But asking them will have a profound effect on your voice. When you begin you will speak or sing directly to those people and they will therefore listen to and hear what you have to say. The first condition of communication is concern for the person you are trying to reach.

Listen

You listen for silence. Then, during the performance, after each completed point or section of music you will return to that silence as to 'home base' so that the audience has a moment for reflection. One of the great mistakes of presentation is talking all the time. The audience needs periods of silence, it cannot take a constant barrage of sound or information, however beautiful or interesting. In the pauses, the sound and information can be digested. There is no attention without these pauses, this silence. The patterns of sound and silence create a rhythm necessary for concentration. Recognise that silence while you listen as a useful tool to enhance your voice. In those periods of silence you will once again STOP and *observe your audience*.

Be alert

You are already halfway there by standing still for a moment on two feet, looking and listening. Chapter One contains a set of exercises which loosen the joints and wake up the vocal trampoline. There are various stretches which accompany singing in this book and the combination of working on these and learning to use the two balance boards will enable you to stand at your full height and width without stiffening. The imagining of the plant pot on your head and the balance board under your feet will send your head up, your heels down and your shoulders away from each other.

You are now concentrating on yourself and observing the audience. In the moment when these two activities occur you will automatically begin to communicate your material because the conditions for good communication have been set up for you. You have already made a connection between your audience and yourself. Your material will flow along this connection in the best possible way for *now*. These are also the conditions which the voice requires for maximum efficiency and quality.

Your voice will have quality, imagination and range because you are balanced and the vocal trampoline is alert and springy.

You are in the best condition for efficient recall, and gradually, when you realise how much stability and confidence these simple procedures give you, you will throw away your notes.

This whole chapter is about one small moment, the moment when the connection between the giver and the receiver is realised. It is the moment when you, as the presenter, walk in with the package, look around the room and say 'I have something here quite wonderful and it is for you.' The carriage and alertness of the bearer tells the audience that the package is special. The attention and where it is directed, looking and listening, tell your listeners whether or not it is for them . . . or the clock at the back of the hall.

Here are some ways to rehearse

1   Face the wall, about a foot away from it, feet apart. Place your hands on the wall, out to the side, fingers 'hanging'. Releasing your ankles, lower your

forehead on to the wall. This will create a new listening to yourself and you will use your back as a sounding board for your voice as you speak and sing. (Keep your eyes open.)

2 Use a balance board and rehearse your song, or speech, while standing on it. The wobble board is good, the balance board better. Try them both. They stop the 'hopping from foot to foot' which many people do, and which unnerves the audience. This also helps you to drop the weight into bum and heels.

3 Rehearse with a towel over your head. This is particularly good for rehearsing very dramatic or emotional material. It is easy to become too personally involved and then your best intelligence suffers and the communication thread is broken. Sounds crazy, but it is very effective. It is impossible to become nervous with a towel over your head. You will then hear the material as the writer/composer intended it without you putting in your penn'orth.

4 Never forget that your back is the sound board for your voice. The sound will only carry to the whole of your audience if you encourage the 'back and down' qualities in your voice which you have experienced in exercise 17, page 145, singing in prone; singing with forehead on the wall, on pages 142–3; being a ventriloquist, page 75, and generally by maintaining a flexible and efficient tongue (see Chapter Three 'Dealing with Words').

Of course the ideal way to rehearse these procedures is to gather a few friends together with some cheese and wine (for afterwards – the voice loses its spring *very* quickly through alcohol: never be tempted to gain Dutch courage with a little glass of something). Then

Thinking of back and down

Look back at the photographs of Thomas singing out of tune and on his balance board. Can you see the same 'trying' in Huw (see page 177) as he delivers his presentation and how much more attractive he becomes when taking risks on his balance board?

swap turns of making a speech, singing a song, reading aloud, saying a poem. Experiment with the balance board and a plant pot and standing, forehead on wall, to address those behind you. It is not only good fun it is good work, and through observation it will teach you a great deal about both voices *and* performing. You may never panic again.

EXERCISE • *Using a bean bag*

If you do rehearse with friends one of the best performance exercises I know is to throw a bean bag backwards and forwards from audience to performer. It teaches you to focus quickly, sharpens your wits and prevents you from becoming boring. Usually when we do this on courses the presenter, or singer, discovers a completely new idea about expressing words, less formal, more natural. People often change the vocabulary of their speech quite dramatically and discover their ability to recall what they have rehearsed. Try it.

Practise with your forehead on the wall or a towel over your head will convince you that a stable head produces a more useful voice. Correct the head wagging habit by putting a bean bag on your head. A bean bag has enough weight to stimulate the spring in the spine but it does not fall off easily, so you do not stiffen.

How is your telephone voice?

If you cannot be seen, it is even more important that your voice expresses the flexibility and quality which the work in the book should now be encouraging. How many times do you answer the phone and make yourself 'comfortable' as Dominic is doing in the second photograph?

When the telephone rings he is concentrating on his typing, obviously absorbed in what he is doing. He then gradually loses this attention during the conversation on the phone. The lack of attention can be seen in the whole body as he gradually slides down the telephone cord, neck sagging, head falling, as though the voice on the other end were gradually hypnotising him. He may be giving out all the information requested, but the voice itself will be

saying 'don't bother with this conversation.' When he puts the phone down the person on the other end may find it very difficult to remember any of the information because of the lack of quality in its delivery. This may result in incorrect note-taking on the information given. Later there may even be a complaint . . . 'But I was told . . .'.

A disconnected voice is difficult to listen to.

Fortunately for his company, Dominic's back reasserts itself the next time he answers the phone. He places two feet firmly on the floor and remembers the invisible plant pot on his head. He frees his jaw, focuses his eyes and widens his face by toning up on those lateral face muscles. Many receptionists have to say an introductory phrase. Now you do not have to 'try' to make it sound interesting. Your voice will do it for you.

Voice now disconnected   *That's better!*

EXERCISE • *Work on preparing a presentation*

Devise a work programme to prepare a presentation. I will leave the subject to you. You know where you are going and what you have to deal with. There are many more ways of approach since you worked on 'Come, Sleep'. Shall I remind you again?

1 Balance yourself.
2 No taking a breath (in case you've lived in a state of emergency all day).
3 Work on moving between speech and singing at will.
4 Bring in your main material but retain your balance with the boards and the plant.
5 Observe your progress then use your imagination to select any exercises in the book which will free the jaw, spring the pelvic floor, free the legs, remove interference from the face muscles, prevent a regression into sucking, etc., etc. You work it out. Use your notebook to plan it.

Nervousness

When we become excited, more adrenalin flows into the bloodstream. If we wish to achieve a peak of efficiency the flow of adrenalin is both necessary and helpful. Adrenalin stimulates the whole nervous system and encourages clearer observation, sharper listening and a more alert vocal trampoline. However, this peak of alertness and competence, aided by the flow of adrenalin, is often mistaken for an emergency situation. Both are responses to dealing with unusual situations; both produce extra energy. There is, in fact, only one small activity which makes the difference between maintaining your stability in dealing with a prepared situation or going all out in every possible way to get yourself out of trouble: a sharp intake of breath.

So, when you come to the day of your performance and you have what you call 'the butterflies', welcome them. The brain and body are preparing you for an excitement which will assist your performance. Without that adrenalin you would not be as alert, as sharp, as co-ordinated. What you must definitely *not* do is walk out to meet that audience, feel that stomach churning and take a deep breath. Instead, ignore the people who are desperately insisting that you *'relax'*. Be afraid, by all means, but allow the fear to go on while you apply yourself to:

ONE   TWO   THREE   FOUR

ONE: **STOP** . . .   moving, planning, thinking, remembering, worrying, organising.

TWO: **OBSERVE** . . .   the audience, the hall, the distances, the spaces, the atmosphere, even the colours on the walls, the clothes people are wearing.

THREE: **LISTEN** . . .   to the silence.

FOUR: **BE ALERT** . . .   stretch yourself between an imaginary pot on your head and the balance board under your feet. Keep your feet alive and working. Feel the width across your back, the spring in your tongue – all those connections which you have strengthened while stuck between Junctions 31 and 32 on the M25.

Now you are ready to sing, recite, act, present, deliver, promote, sell. You have all the necessary facilities at your disposal – so play with them and enjoy yourself.

12

Sandy

S andy stammers, or maybe he stutters. To the person trying desperately to speak, the distinction is purely academic. Whatever you call it, the misery which it brings into your life is almost impossible to bear, but, as with deafness and the nervous twitch, stammering is frequently laughed at.

My brother stammered. He was much older than me so I did not know of any agony it brought him. I remember Mother saying 'Come on, Mick, spit it out' on occasions, but he was never upset by that, or at least I was not aware of it. I also remember that it was a family joke that Mick went to a special school for stammerers when he was young and came back stammering much better than when he went. Apart from this experience I had never really thought about stammering except when I was embarrassed by waiting for an unfortunate victim to get around his blocked speech. I believe this to be a fairly typical level of awareness.

My experience of stammering was changed by a phonecall from Sandy. He rang me from Glasgow asking if he could come to Norfolk to see me. That is a long way to travel to have a voice lesson. The phone call took all of ten minutes, although the arrangements were simply and quickly made. It was only the sense of someone's presence that prevented my putting the phone down before he managed to speak.

He came for a weekend and in two days I learned a great deal about stammering from Sandy. So often stammering is associated with nervousness, lack of confidence, insecurity. But the six foot four inches young man striding down the platform in Norwich displayed none of this.

His father and mother were caring, loving parents and as a child Sandy was bright, mischievous, alert and strong. When he was quite small he was taken sailing in the family boat around the Western Isles. He developed a natural flair for boats and the sea and as he grew he was able to crew in races and, indeed, sail while others crewed for him. Within this happy, stable life Sandy began to stammer at five years old.

I met him aged 22 and by then the stammer had developed such strength that at times there was nothing he could say without struggle, fear and embarrassment. There was little chance of anyone understanding him who was not familiar with this particular struggle or who was not prepared for the facial contortions speech produced. There seemed no reason for him to stammer, no emotional shock, no unhappiness, only lots of love and care from everyone he had grown up with.

On that weekend I encouraged him to talk as much as possible so that I could observe this stammer: when it happened, whether there was any recognisable pattern to it. As he talked I learned that:

> stammering is very common. I had not noticed that, but then I never realised how many people

sang out of tune until I joined them. There are stammering self-help groups all over the country which meet to try to find a way to communicate and relieve the stress for each other. Sandy ran one such group in Glasgow.

2 Sandy believed that stammering was impossible to cure; at least, according to his experience, it certainly seemed so.

Let us look at his record, which I believe is fairly typical.

Throughout his school life he had been to numerous speech therapists and speech 'experts'. He was sent to a child psychologist to check for emotional upset or trauma and was found to be quite normal. A number of private speech treatments were tried, some of them offering miraculous cures, some charging enormous amounts of money – which his parents were more than willing to pay. Some of these 'treatments' actually made his stammer worse.

Sandy was getting older. He resorted more and more (little wonder) to written communication and to those subjects which did not demand much voice work. He obtained very good school results in sciences and went to university where the idea was again broached of Sandy beginning a new set of 'treatments'. By and large he got down to studying and work which could be done without talking. For a time his life was reasonably stable while he got on with stammering and studying. A car accident rendered him completely speechless, so he was examined for nerve damage and given co-ordination tests. Nothing was found except seat belt bruising.

Sailing was now his relief from an environment in

which he felt vocally ill-equipped. He was now racing bigger and bigger yachts. He could be himself on a boat and excelled as a racing helmsman.

When he left university all the world of verbal communication flooded in and again he had to be with other people. He knew that trying to hide his stammer was possible sometimes but that the effort required left him mentally and physically tense. Realising more and more what a social handicap this was and being torn between wanting to speak to people and avoiding situations out of fear, he decided that he must do something himself. He decided firstly to investigate any possible system which claimed to help speech and secondly, to find in one of those systems a means of coping with his disability.

However, he found that he was physically tense after 18 years of continual stammering so he sought first a technique which would give him more control of himself. He had Alexander lessons.

It is imperative that you, as the reader of this book on voices, know all this background. It is important for your own work on your own voice. If you decide really to commit yourself to discovering your vocal potential, there will be times when you will want to throw in the towel. You will become angry because your voice, which you are familiar with and used to, will maybe change. 'I'm not going to pull *my* face about like that when I sing. I may stick like it!' You will become angry with yourself, angry with the book, angry, most of all, with me. When you read the background to the work Sandy has done, what he had endured for 18 years, you begin to understand how strong the voice is, what an important part of us is in operation when we talk or sing. You may not stammer or have any problem at all with your voice, but everything you know about voices, what they do and how they do it, may not only improve you but you may have a Sandy in your family sometime. Instead of panicking and making the child nervous you may be able to help.

I observed Sandy all that weekend. We walked the dogs, he joined in with the family, and together we explored what he could and could not do with his voice.

This is what I observed.

- He could not sing a note and could not remember ever doing so.
- His voice pitch dropped considerably after he had made 'drain noises',
- He took a big breath in order to speak.
- He had never attempted to speak in a voice or a language which was not his own.

He was never given parts in plays and did not take languages at school, except for a struggled German O-level, taken as a scientific requirement. I suppose the theory was that he had enough trouble speaking English without creating more problems.

He admitted to wishing that he could be a newsreader, a great actor, or a linguist, but believed that it was merely because those things were out of reach – 'the moth for the star'.

He had tremendous courage. Whatever I asked him to do as an experiment he did without hesitation, willing to pull his tongue and face into unusual positions to talk, to put pots on his head and sing totally out of tune to stimulate muscles which were not working at all. He wanted to have a normal, communicative life which he had never really had.

What did 'normal life' mean to Sandy? Answering the telephone without fear, ordering a pint at a busy bar, buying a ticket, having one interview for the job he wanted in which he could express how able he was, chatting up a girl, joining in conversations, having one day onshore that was not frustrating, at least part of the time.

We have worked for two years. The voice is richer, fuller, deeper, and it now sings. Sandy has joined a local amateur operatic society. The stammering is reducing in frequency in direct relation to the development of the other qualities. His work on Alexander Technique has taught him how to work through frustration and failure without being defeated by them. His shoulders are less tense and he does not contort himself to speak. It will still take a while to replace 18 years of 'knowing how to stammer' with a programme of 'choosing not to stammer' because the voice is connected to the whole person and so the work has to soak in over a long period of time. It is much easier to change the way that someone runs or uses a tool, even a tool like a violin. All the work we have done and the information we have used is in this book. Some of the work was particularly useful to Sandy as a stammerer and that is worth noting.

When Sandy stammers his tongue, soft palate and jaw shoot forward, the lips pouting in a strong sucking action. This is becoming controlled by strengthening the work of the muscle styloglossus which pulls the tongue backwards and upwards. At first he had no contact with this muscle and it did not operate in his speech.

As you have seen (pages 107–9), there is a dramatic change in the position of both tongue and larynx around the age of six. From two to six the tongue lies entirely in the mouth to form the anterior wall of the throat; the larynx drops to allow for this. Most children talk before six. Sandy was very bright and would obviously learn to express himself very quickly. He could read quite well at five. He learned to do all this with his tongue in a sucking position. Then the tongue and larynx shifted position, which may have given him some adjustment trouble. He did not want to lose any of the progress of talking more and more and better and better about all the fascinating new things he was learning. It may be that he did not allow that adjustment. Perhaps his tongue is still struggling to talk in a sucking position. As Sandy is strengthening the muscle which suspends his tongue backwards and upwards from the floor of the skull, his tongue is beginning to articulate in quite a different position in his throat, not in his mouth at all, and the stammering is becoming controllable. This is apparently in direct relation to the strengthening of the styloglossus muscle – the one tongue muscle not in operation when he was learning to speak.

Perhaps this information on the shift in the tongue and larynx at such an early age is an important consideration in the teaching of all aspects of language. Concessions could then be made for any lack of progress in reading aloud oral class work and pronunciation during this time. Children between the ages of five and eight may have to pause, whenever they have a difficulty, then wait to discover a different way of saying something which they said very easily last week. If that time to stop is not granted to them they may well panic, snatch a breath and block the adjustment. That *could* be the beginning of a stammer.

Certainly, it is information which all parents need so that when their small child mispronounces or even makes up its own language they do not give an example of a slowed-down correct pronunciation and get the child to practise fragments of words out of context, but they just do lots of singing with the child, even in another language. Most people know 'Frère Jacques'. Keep up the singing until the problem goes away. I believe that in the majority of cases it would. When the problem has gone still keep up the singing.

13

Your Tape

Side one

You will find that each exercise on tape refers you to the number of the exercise in the book, which gives instructions and notes. If you take a little time to relate the exercises to work in different chapters you will discover that when you begin to use your tape in the car these exercises will act as keys to unlock all the rest of the information you have read. This is an ideal way to stimulate recall and gradually you will begin to understand how differently the systems of memory and recall operate in you. This, in turn, will help you to dispense with a script when making a speech or the notation when performing a song.

You have only three instructions to follow in order to work completely successfully with this tape.

1   Listen, and read the notes in the book, carefully.
2   Sing or speak where and when it is expected of you.
3   Use the book and tape as often as you can without making it into a chore.

May I remind you that 'successful' is not the same as 'right' or 'correct'? 'Incorrect', 'out of tune' and plainly excrutiating are also successful as events in the rhythmic patterns of learning. Your ear will co-operate with your voice to use this information for improvement if you will only allow it. Off you go, and good luck!

Side two

Sing these songs for fun! To help you to give priority to the vowels, the first line of each English song is written in open-ended syllables. The Italian song, Russian song and Spiritual are entirely written that way. It would be a good exercise for you to complete the rest of each song yourself. You would sing them more easily.

Songs

Send in the clowns

Isn't it rich? Are we a pair?

IZ — ER — NTI — TRI — (CH) AR — WI — AH — PER —

Me here at last on the ground,

ME — HERE — AH — TLA — STO — NTHER — GROUND

You in mid-air.
Send in the clowns.

Isn't it bliss? Don't you approve?
One who keeps tearing around, one who can't move . . .
Where are the clowns? Send in the clowns.

Just when I'd stopped opening doors,
Finally knowing the one that I wanted was yours,
Making my entrance again with my usual flair,
Sure of my lines,
No-one is there.

Don't you love farce? My fault, I fear.
I thought that you'd want what I want.
Sorry, my dear.
But where are the clowns? Quick, send in the clowns.
Don't bother, they're here.

Isn't it rich, isn't it queer,
Losing my timing this late in my career?
And where are the clowns?
There ought to be clowns.
Well, maybe next year . . .

My lord, what a mornin'

I call this your 'special occasion' song. It is for those special occasions when the car in front hasn't moved for twenty minutes, you have had a row with your nearest and dearest, the washing machine has packed up.

My Lord what a mornin'

MAH – LAW – DWO – TAH – MOR – NI – (N)
   [3 times]

When de stars begin to fall,

WE – NDAH – STAR – ZBI – GI – NTOO – FOR – (L)

When de stars begin to fall.

Verse: Done quit all my worldly ways
          Joined dat heabenly band   [Repeat]

Lascia ch'io pianga

1 As it looks:

Lascia ch'io pianga, mia cruda sorte
E che sospiri la libertà!
E che sospiri, e che sospiri la libertà!
Lascia ch'io pianga mia cruda sorte,
E che sospiri la libertà!

Il duolo infranga queste ritorte
De' miei martiri sol per pietà
De' miei martiri sol per pietà.

2 How it sounds:

LA – SCIA – CH'IO – PIA – NGA, MIA – CRU – DA – SOR – TE E – CHE –
SO – SPI – RI, LA – LI – BER – TA,
[repeated]
I – LDUO – LOI – NFRA – NGA, QUE – STE – RI – TOR – TE DE – MIEI –
MAR – TI – RI – SO – LPER – PIE – TA
[repeated]

3 What it means:

Leave me to weep

Let me weep over this, my cruel lot
And contemplate my abandonment.
I made the sacrifices out of pity for you
And the pain of it has broken the bond between us.

'Swonderful!

'Swonderful, 'Smarvellous,

SWO – NDER – FU – (L) SMAR – VE – LER – (S)

You should care for me.

YOO – SHU – DCARE – FOR – ME.

'Sawful nice 'Sparadise
'Swhat I love to see!
You've made my life so glamorous,
You can't blame me for feeling amorous.
Oh, 'Swonderful! 'Smarvellous!
That you should care for me!

'Swonderful! 'Smarvellous!
You should care for me!
'Sawful nice 'Sparadise!
'Swhat I love to see!
My dear, it's four-leaf clover time,
From now on my heart's working overtime.
Oh, 'Swonderful! 'Smarvellous!
That you should care for me!

You can sing the second verse sometimes.

Drink to me only

Drink to me only with thine eyes

DRI – NKTOO – MI – O – NLY – WI – THAH – NAH – ZAR –

And I will pledge with mine,

NDAH – WI – LPLE – JWI – THMAH – (N).

Or leave a kiss within the cup,
And I'll not ask for wine.
The thirst that from the soul doth rise
Doth ask a drink divine,
But might I of Jove's nectar sup
I would not change for thine.

Russian folk song

1 As it looks

Катюша

Расцветали яблони и груши,
Поплыли туманы над рекой.
Выходила на берег Катюша,
На высокий, на берег крутой

2 How it sounds

RA – STVYE – TA – LEE YA – BLO – NEE EE GROO – SHEE

PO – PLI – LEE TOO – MA – NI NA – DRE – KOY.

VWI – HO – DEE – LA NA BE – RE – KA – TYOO – SHAA,

NA VWI – SO – KI, NA BE – RE – KROO – TOY.

3 What it means
The apple and pear-trees were in bloom,
Mist floated over the river.
Katyusha came out onto the bank,
Onto the high, steep bank.

Poems

Sunday morning

Down the road someone is practising scales,
The notes like little fishes vanish with a wink of tails,
Man's heart expands to tinker with his car
For this is Sunday morning, Fate's great bazaar;
Regard these means as ends, concentrate on this Now,
And you may grow to music or drive beyond Hindhead anyhow,
Take corners on two wheels until you go so fast
That you can clutch a fringe or two of the windy past,
That you can abstract this day and make it to the week of time
A small eternity, a sonnet self-contained in rhyme.

But listen, up the road, something gulps, the church spire
Opens its eight bells out, skull's mouths which will not tire
To tell how there is no music or movement which secures
Escape from the weekday time. Which deadens and endures.

Louis McNiece

How doth the little crocodile

How doth the little crocodile improve his shining tail
And pour the waters of the Nile on every golden scale.
How cheerfully he seems to grin, how neatly spread his claws
And welcomes little fishes in with gently smiling jaws.

Lewis Carroll

Hallowe'en

It's Punkie Night tonight,
It's Punkie Night tonight,
Give us a candle, give us a light,
It's Punkie Night tonight.

Hey – how for Hallowe'en
All the witches to be seen,
Some black and some green,
Hey – how for Hallowe'en!

Fee, fi, fo fum,
I smell the blood of an Englishman.
Be he alive or be he dead
I'll grind his bones to make my bread.

Hinx, minx!
The old witch winks,
The fat begins to fry.
There's no one at home
But jumping Joan,
Father, mother and I!

From ghoulies and ghosties,
Long-leggity beasties,
And things that go bump in the night,
Good Lord deliver us.

The Witch! the Witch! don't let her get you!
Or your Aunt wouldn't know you the next time she met you!

Eleanor Farjeon

Come, sleep

Come, Sleep, and with thy sweet deceiving
Lock me in delight awhile.
Let some pleasing dream beguile all my fancies
That from thence I may feel an influence
All my powers of care bereaving.
Though but a shadow, but a sliding,
Let me know some little joy.
They that suffer long annoy
Are contented with a thought
Through an idle fancy wrought.
O let my joys have some abiding.

John Fletcher

Think of your springs again, all stretched and exercised. The jaw
is free, tongue flexible and, balanced on two feet with a strong